Last thing I remember, I was
Running for the door
I had to find the passage back
To the place I was before
"Relax, " said the night man,
"We are programmed to receive.
You can check-out any time you like,
But you can never leave!

The Eagles Hotel California

I, I can remember (I remember)
Standing, by the wall (by the wall)
And the guns shot above our heads
And we kissed,
as though nothing could fall
And the shame was on the other side
Oh we can beat them, for ever and ever
Then we could be Heroes,
just for one day.

David Bowie Heroes

First published in United Kingdom in 2016

# ZAHAL ; A LOVE STORY

# LIFE IN THE ISRAELI ARMY

## JOHNNY WALLMAN

This book is dedicated to Stuart Polley who fell before the end, to Zvi Springman, an inspiration, to Stella and Ossi Vernik who helped build the country from a swamp, to Joanne and Todd and Jeremy and Ian who held my hand as I held theirs and to every Israeli that helped me when I mispronounced a Hebrew word.

The Soundtrack

Zahal : A Love Story

We rode our cycles
Through the streets of naivety
Built castles and dungeons
To protect our hopes and dreams

We watched our heroes
Grace the football field in sky blue
Sang till our voices were gone
An allegiance forever binding and true

We walked the protests and rallies
Donned the badges of our cause
Swore we'd fight till we were heard
Object at the ease our leaders war

We emptied our pockets
Of the hopes and dreams and naivety
Innocence, a casualty of time
When words only had one meaning
We rode our tanks through the streets of occupation
Destroyed castles and bunkers To protect our hopes and
dreams.

I looked about me. My cigarette smoke drifted up from behind my newspaper. My body present, my soul absent. I heard the clatter of coffee cups on saucers. I heard the chatter of middle class banality. I heard them talking to one another in murmurs and whispers. They talked about BMW's, money, the price of everything and the value of nothing. Suddenly I had a vision of the face of destiny. It frightened me. Maybe it was not they who were to blame. No one ever helped them to escape. Like termites, they had built their peace by blocking up with shit every nook and cranny through which any light might enter. They rolled themselves up into a protective ball in their refined security, in routine, in the suppressive conventions of a tedious life, failing to raise even a modest fight against the winds and the tides of a true life.

They had chosen not to be worried by great problems. They had not the time to ask themselves questions to which there seemed no answers. Nobody had grasped them by the shoulder while there had still been time. And now the clay of which they were shaped had cast and hardened, and too late in them would ever awaken the dormant musician, the poet, the artist that perhaps had lived inside them in the beginning. This was not me, this would not be me.

# Introduction When You're Young

In May 1991 my son, Aaron, was born in Manchester, England.
It was time to clear out the junk to make space for a cot, pram
and other essential baby products. Stored in the attic of my
house was my I.D.F. Kit bag packed with my army pants, shirt
and black beret. Five years after I had finished my service and
returned to England from Israel I was ready and prepared for
the call-up if needed. Why the Israeli army would even
consider such a move never entered my head. I am not certain
if I genuinely believed I may be needed or if I just couldn't
empty the bag of the memories.

This is the story of a journey. An English Jew with no religious
convictions who followed his Zionist ideals that called for a
state for the Jewish people. For over two thousand years Jews
throughout the world had striven for their ultimate goal, Aliya,
the coming up, the return to Zion. Following their exile by the
Romans the Jews of the world had just one dream, their return
to the Holy Land. The religious Jews would wait for the
Messiah to bring them back while the survivors of the Nazi
Holocaust felt the need to return too urgent to wait for any
messiah.

Like many secular Jews around the world, I felt a strong bond
with the state of Israel. We were not a religious family. We did
the nominal synagogue days of New Year and Yom Kippur.
My parents kept kosher but worked Saturdays. They were
strong supporters of Israel. We first visited in 1974, the year
after the Yom Kippur War. I don't know if that was a
deliberate act of solidarity with the Jewish State. The previous
year we had taken a family holiday in Cyprus months before
the Turks had invaded. Maybe if they had not invaded and

bombed our hotel in Famagusta we would have revisited and I would never have visited Israel. I remember that first visit with great fondness. I was just eleven years old. I remember camping at The Galilee with my family and the two soldiers, David and Ezra, we had met hitchhiking. It was on this first trip and subsequent visits we met our uncle Zvi Springman. A paratrooper, his parachute failed to open during one combat mission and he was paralysed from the waist down. His strength and courage remained an inspiration. We had quite a few relatives in Israel. When my great grandparents fled the pogroms of Russia at the turn of the nineteenth century, while my grandfather, as a small child, made his way with his family to Britain, others in the family headed for the Holy Land. Sadly my grandfather was never reunited with his first cousin Dov, as he passed away just a month before their planned reunion in Israel.

I spent my early teenage years heavily involved in the Zionist youth movement, more, initially, to gain friends than to work for Israel. We had just moved house and I had moved to high school. Friends were a little thin on the ground. Ian, the older brother of one of my two remaining friends Elyse, was involved in a group called The Federation of Zionist Youth. Before I knew it I was Aliya Officer on a committee with Elyse, Simon, Dave and a few others. A year later I was Chairman.


November 20th 1977 Peace in our time

I remember my father sat in his chair watching the news. We were being particularly noisy as he barked for us to be quiet. 'This is history, this is peace for Israel' he shouted. President Sadat's plane had landed at Ben Gurion airport at the start of his 36-hour visit. He was greeted by Israel's Prime Minister Menachim Begin and Israeli President Ephraim Katzir and a 21-gun salute was fired in his honour.

After the ceremony at the airport President Sadat was driven to Jerusalem for an hour-long meeting with Mr Begin. Sadat addressed the Israeli parliament, the Knesset, with his speech broadcast live to hundreds of millions of people all over the world, our family included. He told the Israeli parliament: 'We really and truly welcome you to live among us in peace and security.'Talks started in Israel in November and eventually led to the Camp David agreement in March 1979. President Sadat's overtures to Israel made him popular in the West - he and Menachim Begin were jointly awarded the Nobel Peace Prize in 1978.But he was isolated and snubbed in the Arab world. In October 1981 he was assassinated by soldiers at a military parade in Cairo.

In September 1980 I joined an American study programme in Israel for a year. I spent a year travelling and studying in Israel. At eighteen years old I seemed to find my identity, a purpose. In April 1983 I packed my bags for good, returning to the land of milk and honey. This was not an adventure. This was a new life, a natural progression, a return to the homeland. The following seven years would be the most difficult, the happiest, the most rewarding and the most depressing. Created were friendships and bonds as strong today as they were during the dark days of the army. Dreams were made, dreams were shattered.

This is an account of those days. Some of it set down raw at the time of my leaving Israel, some written in retrospect almost thirty years later. I apologize for any inaccuracies due to the march of time. I arrived in Israel a new citizen, ready to start a new life in the holy land, to serve and protect my new country. But the milk in the land of milk and honey turned sour. The army, the Israel Defence Force, also an occupying force. The army of the people, sometimes also an uncaring army. The self centred politicians, the political stalemates and the deep polarization of the population made assimilation difficult and life mostly confrontational. All that said, I had, and still have friendships that most people could only dream of. I have befriended some of the most inspirational people I have ever met. Jo and Todd and Ian and Jeremy who guided me through the army and my rants afterwards. Stella and Ossi who became my Israeli parents teaching me more about Israel than any book or scholar. There were others, many others.

There is anger. Anger at myself for failing and at Israel for failing me. But there were good times too. I lost my virginity and my naïve innocence but found myself in this desert land. I learned to think, to love, to hate, to laugh and to cry. This was a love affair. I saw Israel as a lover, a soulmate. Before I knew it we were married and once the honeymoon was over, the troubles began. The fights, the arguments, the name calling. Yet we still loved each other and cared for each other deeply. We just couldn't live together. Now, separated for almost thirty years, I still care for her deeply and miss her immensely The scars have mostly faded, the happy memories pushed through.

This book is dedicated to Stuart Polley who fell before the end, to Zvi Springman, an uncle and inspiration, to Stella and Ossi Vernik who helped build the country from a swamp, to Joanne and Todd and Jeremy and Ian who held my hand as I held theirs and to every Israeli that helped me when I mispronounced a Hebrew word.

Welcome to Israel

The history of Israel and Palestine is written by two very different sides with two very different accounts of the same events. Since the days of the bible never the twain have met. The result, a conflict that has caused pain and suffering not only to the people of the region, but murder and mayhem throughout the world. The conflict has given an excuse for Anti-Semitism, Islamophobia and Imperialism, both capitalist and religious, Christian, Jewish and Islamic.

The land area of Palestine refers to the region which lies on the southern Mediterranean coastal plains. On a modern day map Palestine would be Israel, Jordan, Gaza and The West Bank. It cannot be certain on where the term 'Palestine' originates. Historical sources state it is from the term 'Philistines' that the name 'Palestinians' has been taken. The word Palestine is the derivation of 'Plesheth', which meant migratory or rolling. It is generally agreed that there have always been Christians, Jews and Moslems living there. The area has always come under the rule of another power be it Roman, Ottoman or British. It has never been an independent sovereign state. In the kindergarten of world politics it was a football in the playground that nobody had ever owned. When the British ended their rule in 1947, both the Jews and the Arabs claimed the ball for themselves. Both had a legitimate claim having been 'promised' the land at one time or another . Over sixty years later both sides continue the fight.

In 63 BC, Palestine became a territory of the Roman Empire, leading to the dispersal of the Jews and Christians out of Jerusalem. Muslim rule in Palestine began in 638 AD. During the First World War the region came under the control of the

Ottoman Empire, and subsequently the British occupation. In 1917, Britain announced the Balfour Declaration, where the British government declared 'His Majesty's government view with favour the establishment in Palestine of a national home for the Jewish people, and will use their best endeavours to facilitate the achievement of this object.' Two years earlier in an exchange of ten letters between Sir Henry McMahon, Britain's high commissioner in Egypt, and Sharif Hussein bin Ali, Emir of Mecca and King of the Arabs Britain pledged to support Arab independence if Hussein's forces revolted against the Ottomans. British double dealing at its finest. At this time the Jewish population was around 60,000 compared to an Arab population of around 730,000. Britain's formal mandate of the region was formally announced in 1922.

Following the Second World War in 1947, Britain announced their termination of the mandate and left the United Nations with the decision to divide the territory. A recommendation for partition of Palestine between an Arab state and a Jewish state was imposed. This was accepted by Jewish leadership but rejected by the Arab Higher Committee. The Jewish population, bolstered by immigration from war torn Europe and neighbouring Arab countries, had now reached over one million matching the Arab figure.

As the Jews arrived they acquired more land. They built cities along the Mediterranean, Tel Aviv, Netanya. They purchased houses in Arab towns such as Haifa and Jaffa. They, with financial aid from Jews living in America and Europe, bought land from Arab locals and built settlements (kibbutzim). Many of these kibbutzim were next to Arab towns and both sides cooperated well. Many others saw nightly raids and attacks. According to Israel, no Arabs were evicted from their homes and exiled as refugees, around 300,000 left voluntarily to return once the Israeli state had been crushed. According to the Arabs, over 500 Arab villages were taken over by Israel with over 700,000 Palestinian refugees forced over the border into Jordan. Sixty years of arguments, sixty hours of internet searching has failed to give a definitive and true history. Any truth has been horribly lost amongst the occupation of a people and the bombing of innocent citizens.

Days before the establishment of the State of Israel Zionist officials met to decide what the new country would be called. There were three options: Palestine, Zion, and Israel. The three officials were working under two assumptions: That an Arab state was about to be established alongside the Jewish one in keeping with the UN's partition resolution the year before, and that the Jewish state would include a large Arab minority whose feelings needed to be taken into account. They rejected the name Palestine, they wrote, because they thought that would be the name of the new Arab State. They rejected the name Zion, seemingly because the words 'Zion' and 'Zionist' already had a pejorative meaning in the Arab world. Calling the country Zion 'would cause real difficultly for the Arab citizen in the Jewish state,' they said. In the end, they opted for the most straightforward option: Israel.

On May 14th 1948 a homeland for the Jews, Israel, was declared. With this announcement, what had been primarily a civil war between the region's Jewish and Arab populations became an international war. On the night of May 14 - 15, five Arab League countries, Egypt, Iraq, Jordan, Lebanon, and Syria, invaded Israel. Israel's losses in the war for independence were tallied at approximately 1% of its population, 6,373, of which approximately 4,000 were soldiers. The number of Arab losses is estimated at 10,000 — 15,000.

The War proceeded through the rest of 1948 with a series of truces, frequently broken, to the negotiated agreements that ended the war in 1949. Fighting ended with a cease-fire January 7, 1949 and the War of Independence was formally terminated on July 20, 1949 with the signing of the Israel-Syria armistice agreement.

The Israelis had mobilised almost their entire military age population. The imbalance in numbers was very clear, even without considering additional support from Saudi Arabia and other countries allied with the Arab League. The imbalance in war material was even more unfavourable to the Israelis. But the Israelis had the fervour that came from knowing they only had one chance to succeed or die in the attempt. There was no alternative to victory.

The reborn State of Israel was aided by Jewish volunteers from around the world (called the Machal) who left their civilian lives and made their way along a clandestine route to help. Although small in number, about 3500, they were a tremendous asset in skills and morale for the tiny, struggling Israeli military.

Chapter 1 Israel
April 30th 1984


You came from nowhere, journeyed to me
to orchards filled with fruit
and wide open spaces
stretching towards snow covered peaks

Lost in our worlds, hypnotised from the start
A perfect place to hide
from ourselves as much as the crowd
Still, together we banished any lingering doubts

Beyond the gentle stream
The rapids washed away any reservations
Beyond the sunset
Together we found our salvation

Can you see our future
Resting on those snow covered peaks
Will we ever be released from this place
between the river and the trees.

So this was it then. The EL AL Israel airlines 747 gracefully lifted towards 30,000 feet while my heart remained on the wet Manchester airport Tarmac. Having requested a window seat I watched the grey airport fade into the distance. I wondered if, in the great Jewish tradition my mother was still crying at my departure, my father failing desperately to comfort her and my younger siblings shuddering with embarrassment. Also joining the impromptu farewell party were close friends Simon and Dave.

I was excited and nervous. It had taken some time and much thought before deciding on Aliya. I was leaving behind a loving family and a comfortable lifestyle. The plane seat pouch was filled to overflowing with the usual flight magazines and duty free catalogues. I added to the clutter wedging in enough newspapers to fill the time on an transatlantic flight let alone a five hour flight to the Eastern Mediterranean. The real danger would come should I require the sick bag now buried deep into the seat pocket.

I was certain this was the right move but it wasn't easy leaving England. I was unsettled and eager to start afresh in Israel. I felt a purpose. I would miss my family and their security. I would miss my few remaining friends and of course my beloved Manchester City. I did feel a little disloyal leaving them especially after their Saturday defeat at Derby County. If we were to push back into the top flight then maybe I should be there to lend support. Under the management of Billy McNeil and captain Paul Power it looked like another season next year in Division Two and under the awful shadow of United. It had all looked so good until three defeats in April. I felt the guilt of leaving. How could I influence from 2000 miles away? I pulled the newspapers from the seat pocket deciding to create a positive impression by starting with the

Sunday Times. As I lifted the paper from inside fell out a copy of the soft porn magazine 'Penthouse'. So much for impressing the neighbours. With the damage already done I flicked through the magazine. I could feel the warm breath of the man seated next to me as he read over my shoulder. Suddenly I felt a jolt as the force of the man's wife's dig signalled her disdain at her husbands reading material. I decided to avoid any domestic turbulence by putting the magazine away for a rainy day.

I stared from the window, not that there was much to see at 30,000 feet. I fell deep into thought. After my year in Israel I had returned to England stuffed with the glory of Israel. I resented the static lives of my contemporaries in Manchester. My friends had now gone their own way, one to London, one to Leeds and a third to Jersey. My reason for being was not coffee at the Midland Hotel on a Saturday night. My social life truly dead, there was my work. Having recklessly deciding at age twelve that education was not for me I left school with just two o-levels and a budgie. The family grocery business offered an income and a safety net but little more.

Involved with the Federation of Zionist Youth from around age fifteen, in 1980 I joined Year Course, an educational programme run jointly with the American Young Judea. There we spent time on Kibbutz Ketura in the Arava desert, studied at Beit Riklis in Jerusalem and spent a month on Moshav Avigdor near Ashkelon. It was here I met Stella and Ossi Vernik, to this day the two most inspirational people I have ever met. The Israel experience further unsettled me in England and from the day of my return I planned my Israel homecoming. In April 1983 I returned joining an Ulpan to learn Hebrew at Kibbutz Tzuba near Jerusalem. Now, a year later, I was returning as an Israeli citizen having spent a few weeks back in England arranging my Aliya and organising the shipping of my life from Manchester to my new homeland. Now it was all so final.

The plane touched down at Ben Gurion airport in Tel Aviv. The music played as I put on my badge 'I'm coming home'. I felt a bit stupid and childish wearing a badge but it should give me priority access through immigration. It did as a middle aged gentleman escorted me out of the line at passport control taking me through a back door to offices upstairs at the airport. I expected something a little more dramatic and welcoming like a red carpet, brass band and fireworks. To be honest the whole process was a little under-whelming. Within the hour I was an Israeli citizen with my new identity card shielded in a light blue holder with a picture of a menorah and the words 'State of Israel' embossed on the cover. I was given a voucher for a taxi to anywhere in Israel. I was tempted to choose the beach in Eilat, some five hours drive away but elected for Kibbutz Tzuba near to Jerusalem. I was home. It felt strange but good. I was excited. I was 22 years old and had finally made it home and I was about to get laid.

Tel Tzova was the site of an ancient Jewish settlement in the days of King David according to the bible. In 1170, a Crusader fortress, Belmont, was built there to guard the route to Jerusalem. Belmont was conquered by Saladin in 1191. The adjacent Arab village of Suba was the scene of fierce fighting during the 1948 War of Independence due to its strategic location overlooking the road to Jerusalem. In late 1947 and early 1948, irregular forces of the Egyptian Muslim brotherhood stationed in Suba repeatedly attacked Jewish convoys on the main highway from Tel Aviv to Jerusalem. The village was conquered by the Palmach branch of the Israeli army during the night of July 12–13 as part of Operation

Danny. Most of the inhabitants fled before the fighting and did not return. Most moved to Jordan, although some moved only one km away to the nearby village of Ein Rafa where they and their descendants live to this day as Israeli citizens. In October 1948 a group of Palmach veterans established Kibbutz Misgav Palmach 1km south of Suba, which was later renamed Palmach Tzova, also known in English as Kibbutz Tzuba. Around five hundred people lived on Tzuba. Industries included a furniture factory and agriculture consisting of a dairy farm and cotton fields.

## May 12th 1984 Stay With me Till Dawn

With the two hour time difference, listening to the BBC World Service football commentary at 7pm seemed slightly strange. I knew City had lost any chance of promotion following three defeats in April. All that new boss Billy McNeil could do was give the boys a push to impress the Kippax faithful on the last day of the season. I listened in from my kibbutz room as we thumped Cambridge United 5 – 0. Twenty thousand fans cheered at Maine Road, I cheered from the Holy City but alas we finished fourth, a full ten points behind promoted Chelsea, Newcastle and Sheffield Wednesday. The Jews say 'next year in Jerusalem, I said next year in Division One.

My future in Israel had been organized by Reuven, the ulpan manager. The ulpan was a programme where foreigners learned Hebrew half days and worked on the kibbutz the other half. Some were new immigrants like myself but most were Jews from around the world seeking an Israel experience. Although I had my own room I lived mostly with Gila, an New York American who had been living on Kibbutz Tzuba for ten years. She was a few years older than myself and considerably more aware of Israeli life and even more sexually aware. Most weekends were spent studying her favourite book, 'The Joys of Sex'. It was with Gila that I had my second sexual encounter which turned out to be considerably more exciting, and rewarding, than my first a year before. That, the loss of my virginity on Kibbutz Ketura, had been a nervous, less than thrilling event, for either of us.

We were a short bus ride from Jerusalem and visited the city often. A thick steak was always welcome after the buckets of cottage cheese and salad consumed on the kibbutz. The Arab quarter of the 'Old City' was relatively safe with the shuk, or market, stuffed with tempting treats. Beyond the wooden camels and tins of holy air (I know, but people did buy them) were delights from home. Mars bars and Cadbury chocolate were an expensive treat hard to resist. Meanwhile Reuven had organized a meeting for me with the army and in particular, Nahal, a branch of the army where soldiers are based part of the time on kibbutz. With Nahal, soldiers join a garin, a group, usually of people with the same circumstances, maybe school friends, or immigrants with no family in the country. I joined a garin to Kibbutz Kfar Blum situated in the Upper Galilee, close to the northern border with Lebanon. I knew little, if anything, of the make up of the army leaving the choices to Reuven. I knew the Israeli Navy was not an option as I couldn't really swim and hated the sea. To join the air force you had to be much cleverer than I was. Tanks were hot and stuffy. As for artillery, well those shells made rather a loud bang. So Nahal Infantry it was. I would be a paratrooper jumping from planes like my hero Uncle Zvi. Not. The guidelines for how long a new immigrant serves was quite complicated. It was not based on the age of the immigrant but their age when they first settled permanently in the country.

For that reason some, like Alberto, who had first settled in Israel when he was twenty but managed to dodge his call up for fifteen years, finally served three full years like the teen Israelis. He was almost forty when he finally finished. My time would be based on my arrival in April 1983 and my age at the time, twenty one. I would serve two years.

I looked at the Jerusalem hills, the forest stretching down the mountains as the sun set over the golden city. I would miss the beauty of Jerusalem, the walks through the Arab market, the smell of spices and fresh pita bread on the stalls. I felt moved in Jerusalem even though I had no religious feelings. I often sat on what remained of the Belmont Crusader fortress. The view was stunning, the rocky green hills of Jerusalem, the thick forests where most Jews in the diaspora supposedly had trees planted. A common Bar Mitzvah present. Just what a thirteen year old pubescent teenager really wants, a certificate for half a dozen trees in a foreign country.

Jerusalem is located on a plateau in the Judean Mountains between the Mediterranean Sea and the Dead Sea. It is one of the oldest cities in the world It is considered holy to the three major Abrahamic religions. Israelis and Arabs both claim Jerusalem as their capital. Although officially the capital of Israel, all countries around the world refuse to recognise this and house their embassies in Tel Aviv rather than in Jerusalem. Costa Rica and El Salvador became the last two countries to move from Jerusalem to Tel Aviv. During its long history, Jerusalem has been destroyed at least twice, besieged over twenty times, attacked fifty times, and captured and recaptured forty times. The oldest part of the city was settled in 4BC. In 1538 walls were built around Jerusalem under Suleiman. Today those walls define the Old City which has been traditionally divided into four quarters known as the Armenian,

24

Christian, Jewish and Muslim Quarters. Modern Jerusalem has grown far beyond the Old City's boundaries. According to the bible, King David conquered the city and established it as the capital of the United Kingdom Of Israel and his son, King Solomon commissioned the building of the first Temple. In Sunni Islam, Jerusalem is the third-holiest city, after Mecca and Medina. Today, Jerusalem remains one of the core issues in the Israel Palestine conflict. During the 1948 war, West Jerusalem was among the areas captured and later annexed by Israel while East Jerusalem, including the Old City, was captured and later annexed by Jordan. Israel captured East Jerusalem from Jordan during the 1967 Six Day War and subsequently annexed it. Israel's 1980 Basic Law refers to Jerusalem as the country's undivided capital and all branches of the Israeli government are located in Jerusalem, including the Knesset (Israel's parliament), the residences of the Prime Minister and President and the Supreme Court.

This was my last night on Tzuba before my move north. The evening was spent with Shmulik and Dikla, my designated kibbutz family. Neither spoke much English. My Hebrew was relatively poor making conversation somewhat limited. Our enthusiasm carried us through. Since my arrival they had opened their home to me. We had drank Turkish coffee and watched incomprehensible television shows together. The night was spent testing Gila's bed springs. We both knew my departure would bring an inevitable end to our relationship but for now we promised to love each other to the death. Letters had arrived frequently from the old country. Simon kept me informed on the football, Dave, on the soaps, my mother on the family gossip and my father on the staff at work. I wasn't sure if they all thought this odyssey temporary. I felt it wasn't.

So What is a Kibbutz?

Kibbutz literally means gathering or grouping, plural kibbutzim. They are a collective community in Israel that was traditionally based on agriculture. Initial settlers were immigrants with no previous farming experience who drained swamps in the north and turned desert sands into green fields in the south. The first kibbutz, established in 1909, was Degania situated in northern Israel. Today, farming has been partly replaced by other economic branches, including industrial plants and high-tech enterprises. Kibbutzim began as utopian communities, a combination of socialism and Zionism. In recent decades, some kibbutzim have been privatised and changes have been made in the communal lifestyle. A member of a kibbutz is called a kibbutznik. Today some 270 kibbutzim, varying in size from 80 to over 2,000 people, are scattered throughout Israel. With a total population of around 120,000 they represent about three percent of Israel's population. Most kibbutz members work in some section of the kibbutz economy: orchards, factory or dairy. Routine jobs such as dining room duties are rotated among members.

The principle of equality was taken extremely seriously up until recently. Kibbutzniks did not individually own tools, or even clothing. Gifts and income received from outside were turned over to the common treasury. If a member received a gift or had money in a private bank account, it would be turned over to the kibbutz. Up until recently, members ate meals together in the communal dining hall. This was seen as an important aspect of communal life. Members did not receive a wage for work on the kibbutz or own their homes but also did not pay rent on their home nor utility bills.

The ideal was a grand one. A community where everyone was equal, where every job was as important as the next, where everybody worked as hard as the next. The great Socialist ideal that you need a cleaner as much as a doctor. In the early years, and later on the smaller kibbutzim, it worked. But kibbutzim also had their share of members who were not hard workers or who abused common property. Kibbutzim, as small, isolated communities, tended to be places of gossip, exacerbated by lack of privacy and the regimented work and leisure schedules. Many hard working free thinkers left the kibbutz for the city where they could benefit financially and socially. That said up to the late 1970s a disproportionate high number of elite soldiers, artists, authors and politicians all came from the kibbutz.

Many kibbutzim would encourage volunteers, Jewish and non Jewish, to work. Many non Jewish volunteers stayed on afterwards marrying kibbutz members. For myself, the kibbutz was the ideal place for me to start my Israel journey. Unfortunately it was not the ideal place for me to continue it.

Chapter 2 Power in the Darkness

May 21st 1984

Kfar Blum is a kibbutz in the Hula Valley part of the Upper Galilee. Located about 5km south-east of the town of Kiryat Shmona. In 1984 the population was around 600. It was founded in November 1943 by the Labour Zionist Habonim youth movement. The founding members of the kibbutz were primarily from the United Kingdom, South Africa, The United States and Baltic states. The kibbutz was named in honour of Leon Blum, the Jewish socialist former Prime Minister of France who was the focus of a widely publicised, and ultimately unsuccessful show trial in 1942 mounted by the collaborationist Vichy regime.

Agriculture including cotton, dairy and fruit and light industry formed the primary economic basis for the kibbutz. Later this had been supplemented increasingly by tourism. Kfar Blum's location next to the Jordan River at the foot of Mount Hermon made it a centre for outdoor recreational activities including walking, hiking, kayaking and rafting. The kibbutz had a popular and successful hotel/guest house. As with Kibbutz Tzuba, Kfar Blum was not a religious kibbutz. If there was a synagogue on either kibbutz I could not locate them. The difference between Kfar Blum and Tzuba was noticeable. Kfar Blum seemed 'more English' in that with so many members having arrived from English speaking countries, the American class students and the volunteers, one tended to hear English around the kibbutz as much as Hebrew. The difference between Kfar Blum and Ketura, where I had spent six months during Year Course in 1980 was even more stark. Ketura, much smaller in both size and membership, lived by the kibbutz ideals to the letter. Most of the members were American immigrants with strong Socialist views. I remember one wedding when the families of the couple, visiting from abroad, brought wedding gifts such as kettles, blenders and other electrical appliances. The couple were not allowed to keep the gifts as the other members did not have the same items. All money, savings and investments held by a new member were handed to the kibbutz. By contrast, at Kfar Blum many kept their savings in accounts in the bank at Kiryat Shmona. It appeared the only possession really shared were wives and girlfriends.

It was my first week on Kfar Blum. The army, although just three months away, seemed way off in the distance. Weekly garin meetings were held to determine policies, members and a name. I arrived slightly later than most others and many friendships had already formed. I shared a room with Malcolm from London. He had changed his name to Moshe partly due to the fact that Israelis couldn't pronounce Malcolm. 'Mal col um' also had a problem with his surname. Coss, when written in Hebrew, could be read as 'Cus', the lower part of the female body.

We were one of three couples housed outside the main garin building. I use the terms couple and housed in the loosest possible terms. Being away from the main group did sometimes hinder our integration but did provide a welcome respite from the sometimes petty garin politics. Our room was small and very basic. Once inside the small building, to the left a bathroom, the paint having flaked off the walls many years before our arrival. Opposite the entrance there was a small sink and marble worktop. For cooking we were supplied with a hot plate that rarely exceeded a temperature above freezing. This was the kitchen. The bedroom was divided in half by a curtain. Crammed inside my half were my worldly goods shipped from England. It was a challenge. Privacy, not a great characteristic of the kibbutz, was almost non existent. Somehow we managed to avoid killing each other. Next to our room was a bathroom, last painted by the settlers of 1948. The remainder of the group lived in a large building on the other side of the kibbutz. Besides the bedrooms there was a moadon, a communal living room and slightly more advanced kitchen. It was here we would hold our garin meetings, watch the communal television or just relax. .

We were a stones throw, or Ketusha rocket, away from the Lebanon border. To the east was the Golan and a little further east was the Syrian border. The River Jordan ran along the perimeter of the kibbutz. Even with enemies so close there was a peaceful air to the place. The river was perfect for swimming during the hot afternoons, the banks just as useful for horizontal pleasures on hot balmy summer nights. There was, however, some friction between kibbutz and town. Kfar Blum was far more wealthy than the average kibbutz and the members had a higher standard of living than the residents of Kiryat Shmona. The kibbutz, with its Olympic sized swimming pool and football pitch, where the national team had trained, was known as the country club. The kibbutz manufactured sprinkler systems for both domestic and international irrigation. Work in the factory was as thrilling as watching Manchester City eek out a 0-0 draw with Bristol Rovers on an icy, cold Tuesday night. It was a job I managed to avoid opting for the apple orchard instead.

We were the first garin to Kfar Blum. The hope was that once we completed our army service we would return to live on the kibbutz. Nobody knew really where we stood in the hierarchy of the kibbutz structure. I always thought that the kibbutz, a great Socialist experiment, would rise above 'the class system' but it appeared not. We were certainly higher up the greasy pole than the volunteers but well below the kibbutz members. The kibbutz system, supposedly a socialist ideal where every man was equal, seemed to follow the Orwell theme that some are more equal than others. Our roles and what was expected of us were explained by Rita, our Garin/Kibbutz co-coordinator. Promises and commitments were made by both sides, and, for a little while, kept by both sides.

Our democracy was both interesting a a little shaky. While the kibbutz invited garin applicants, the final decision on acceptance was down to us. It was during these, sometimes heated, meetings that personalities shone and allegiances formed. These meetings, chaired by Rita, invariably ended in chaos, wild accusations and a loud brawl. We were supposed to be building bonds between us in readiness for our up coming service, instead we had started war between us.

Shaky democracy was not only the domain of the garin. The nation as a whole had gone to the polls to attempt to elect a new government. This was my first election as an Israeli citizen. I was excited at the prospect of casting my vote. It was strange. I had voted in elections in England and while local issues were important, to me so too was the candidates attitude to Israel. Now I was in Israel, voting in Israel.

The Israeli system of Proportional Representation was aimed at giving all minorities a chance of being heard. Problem was it just didn't work. When a Jew can have an argument in a room of one, there is little hope for agreement in a room of twenty. Every fringe group in Israel fielded candidates during an election. Over twenty five parties stood in the 1984 election. Due to the stalemate produced by the elections, it was decided to form a national unity government, with Labour and Likud holding the leadership for two years each. Labour Shimon Peres formed the twenty-first government in 1984, and as well as Likud, the coalition included the National Religious Party, Agudat Israel, Shas, Morasha, Shinui and Ometz. Aside from national unity governments created at a time of war it was the largest ever government in Israeli political history, with 97 members. Everybody was represented from the almost extreme right to the extreme left. How anything ever got passed was beyond me.

In accordance with the rotation agreement, Peres resigned in 1986 and Likud's Yitzhak Shamir formed the twenty-second government on 20 October 1986. Shinui, a left wing party, resigned from the coalition in May 1987. The Knesset also contained two controversial parties, right wing Kach and left wing Progressive List for Peace. Kach was a far-right party that advocated the expulsion of Israeli Arabs, and although it had run in previous elections, it had not passed the electoral threshold. Ultimately the party was banned after a law was passed barring parties that incited racism. As it turned out my vote for Labour, my first vote in an Israeli election, really didn't count for much. I suppose it did help the party get into power for two years if not for a full term.

One dispute that we constantly failed was any agreement of our garin name. The group was hopelessly split between a serious or a fun name. The more profound name usually offered by Laura, the more ridiculous the name counter offered by Todd. Finally, with little time remaining to deliver our chosen name to the army, Todd proposed 'Nesher', 'Eagle'. Laura was dumbstruck. Finally the boy had used his heart, his head and his sensitivity and offered a beautiful option.

'Yes, that's fantastic' delighted Laura 'The vision of an eagle gliding through the clear blue sky, the power, the grace, the beauty'.

'Well yes that too' replied Todd 'But did you know that when eagles mate they do so in mid air flying towards the ground. The male must finish before they hit the ground because they wont stop. Now that is dedication to the cause.' The room erupted into laughter and total mayhem. Laura now objected to the proposed name but Todd's proposal was carried. We were now Garin Nesher, the group of the eagle.

We were now just two weeks away from our entry into Zahal, the Israeli army and three weeks away from the new football season where again Manchester City would attempt an assault into the top division. This was going to be our year, tough, painful yet successful. One place we were not prepared for sustained pain was on the running track. The kibbutz soccer field was surrounded by a well maintained, Olympic style athletics track. Our aim was to cover several laps in the build up to our army call up. We would raise our pathetic fitness levels and stamina from a starting point of zero. Visit one saw the full compliment of the menfolk and an impressive two circuits of the track, without a stop halfway for a cigarette break. Unfortunately visit two saw just half the guys show up and by visit three the training regime had been abandoned due to lack of interest. As Israeli lack of success at the Olympics have showed, and very limited success on the football pitch have also demonstrated, Jews were not exactly renowned for their athletic or sporting prowess. It wasn't really surprising our attempts to reach a physical peak came to nothing. When Sylvester Stallone starred as John Rambo in the 1982 movie 'First Blood', his character was certainly not based on Johnny Wallman. I had been described as 'slight and puny', somewhat disingenuously but fairly by some observers.

None of us could really have been cast in the movie First Blood. Todd, perhaps came the closest. He looked tough, stocky and well built, although his 1980s porn movie style moustache minimised his limited macho image. Peter came a distant second, tall and lanky, fast around the track, but as clumsy as the rest of us. Jeff was probably the best all rounder, as he proved later. He was of average build and never looked physically tough but during training he managed to take the physical pain much better than the rest of us. Moshe ran like a girl and threw likewise. I worried about standing anywhere within a ten yard area when he threw a hand grenade. Malcolm was the oldest by some years. He was short and stocky with a chest so hairy it would have made any rug maker envious. On rare occasions he would be spotted without a roll-up cigarette perched on his lip. His talent I admired most was his ability to roll a cigarette with just one hand. We called Malcolm 'Grandad'. Kenny was fat. He was grossly over weight and even more obnoxious. As we all related past jobs and experiences it appeared that whatever we had done, he had done too for a couple of years. We calculated that, taking into account all the jobs he had done over the years, he was about 150 years old.

The girls of the garin were as diverse as the menfolk. Laura seemed to take control especially during garin meetings. Yael, by contrast, petite and sweet, never complained nor uttered a cross word. With the exception of Kenny on the guys side, the men bonded pretty well. Unfortunately on the female side, it seemed like conflict from the first day. Susan was slim and beautiful, Jo was slim, beautiful and sexy and smart. They were funny and joked often with the guys. They turned heads where Janet and Yaffa didn't. I don't know if Janet and Yaffa had some kind of inferiority complex about Jo and Susan, even at my advanced age I still struggle with female psychology. There always seemed to be conflict between the four. I often felt uncomfortable as I tried to remain friendly with all four. Later, after Susan left the garin, Janet, very unfairly, went for the jugular with Jo. I finally lost my impartiality.


Chapter 3 Boys of Summer

August 13th 1984

The eve of the war, or at least the eve of our departure to the army and in time honoured ceremony the males of the pack gathered at the shores of the River Jordan to get well and truly wasted. Grown men openly wept as pledges of love and honour were passed as liberally as the beers. All things considered, and probably more out of necessity, we had bonded pretty well. There were shirkers, Kenny for one, but for now we were all eagles, special forces, friends that would carry each others pain, For that night anyway. Few on the kibbutz slept that night with most suffering our drunken singing. I thought of my family back in Manchester, of all our families from Manchester to New York. They too knew our hour was close. They must have been terrified yet hopefully proud. Maybe this was what I really wanted, to finally make my family proud of me. The girls kept their distance during our party. They would not be enlisting for another three months. This was our stag night.

The alcohol numbed a few of the nerves but I was still terrified. I wanted to live here in Israel, to become a citizen and assimilate into society. The army was that tool. Everybody did it. There had been many before and surely many to come after. For so long my mind had been nomadic while many of my friends around me seemed to follow a path. I saw others who, in Manchester, were stagnant, leading boring, humdrum lives. I hated that. There was a world out there to be discovered and the furthest they had travelled was felafel in Rusholme, Manchester. I wanted felafel from the source. I had drifted from one skyline, one sunset to another. Here in Israel I think I had found my inner peace, I had found my home.

I sat on the river bank, the moonlight and stars the only illumination. The singing drowned out the noise of the water crashing over the rocks. I threw a stick into the river and watched it ride the flow. For a few moments I was lost inside myself, oblivious to the noise around. Of course the party ended with a brawl. I missed the start but Kenny must have made some inappropriate comment, again, causing several around him the expression of a few home truths. We were in for a bumpy ride. I stumbled back to my room. I hadn't been this drunk in a long time. I needed to throw up but it wouldn't come. I passed the volunteers rooms. They were still partying but then they always did They never seemed to sleep. I was frightened for tomorrow. I more fell into bed than climbed. The noise of my shoes hitting the floor woke Ruth. She opened her eyes and gave me an understanding smile. She held out her welcoming arms and I collapsed into them. We kissed and then made love like two lovers who would never see each other again. In all reality I would probably be back in two days but who knew what would happen in war?

Zahal, The Israel Defence Force

The Israel Defence Force 'The Army of Defence for Israel', commonly known in Israel by the Hebrew acronym Zahal. They consist of the ground forces, air force, and navy. An order from Defence Minister David Ben-Gurion on 26 May 1948 officially set up the Israel Defence Forces as a conscript army formed out of the paramilitary group Haganah, incorporating the militant groups Irgun and Lechi. The number of wars and border conflicts in which the IDF has been involved in its short history makes it one of the most battle trained armed forces in the world. While originally the IDF operated on three fronts, Lebanon and Syria in the north, Jordan and Iraq in the east, and Egypt in the south, after the 1979 Egyptian–Israeli Peace Treaty, it concentrated its activities in southern Lebanon and the Palestinian Territories. National military service is mandatory for all Israeli citizens over the age of 18, although Arab, but not Druze, citizens are exempted if they so please, and other exceptions may be made on religious, physical or psychological grounds. Men served three years in the IDF, women two years.

After personnel complete their regular service, they are either granted permanent exemption from military service, or assigned a position in the reserve forces. The IDF may call up reservists for duty during conflict or reserve service of up to one month every three years, until the age of 40 or 45. Reservists may volunteer after this age. This was the theory but in practice I served three months and dodged a fourth in the space of less than two years. In most cases, the reserve duty was carried out in the same unit for years, in many cases the same unit as the active service and by the same people. Many soldiers who served together in active service meet in reserve duty for years after their discharge. Defence expenditures increased dramatically after both the 1967 and 1973 wars. They reached a high of about 24% of GDP in the 1980s. Around 100,000 Israelis reach military age annually with around 150,000 active personnel and 400,000 reserve personnel.

The Nahal Infantry Brigade is one of the Israel Defence Forces main infantry brigades. It was established in 1982. Nahal Infantry Brigade soldiers undertake around four months of basic training and around four months of advanced training in the Israeli desert. It operates on the most volatile Israeli borders, Lebanon, Syria and Gaza as well as in the West Bank territories. It is tasked with regular patrol and observation operations on the borders, counter-terrorist operations and riot control in the West Bank. It has operated in all major wars and large-scale operations since its inception, playing key roles during the First and Second Lebanon War and the First and Second Intifada.

Without our role in bringing down its reputation, The Nahal Brigade did not command the same high respect of its rivals Golani and Givati infantry brigades. The training, basic and advanced, was as tough and rigorous but the civilian perception was that with Nahal soldiers serving six months of their service on kibbutz, picking fruit in an orchard was hardly comparable with battle or battle training. On the night of 25th November 1987, two Palestinians took off from Southern Lebanon, each armed with an AK-47 assault rifle, a pistol with a silencer, and several hand grenades. Their gliders were each powered by lawn mower size engines. The engine noises were heard by several soldiers, and the Israeli Northern Command was alerted to the danger of an infiltration. An alarm was sounded, flares were fired and helicopters were sent out to search for the gliders, but without success, as the gliders were flying as low as tree level. However, at the Gibor army camp, about two miles east of Kiryat Shmona, no security precautions had been taken thirty minutes after the alarm was issued and no additional guards had been posted at the camp's gate.

One glider landed in the security zone as a result of being blinded by the searchlights from Kibbutz Ma'ayan Baruch, and the terrorist was tracked down and killed by Israeli troops. The second landed near the Gibor camp. The second terrorist spotted a passing army truck outside the base and opened fire on it, killing the officer driving it. He then headed towards a nearby army encampment manned by Nahal Brigade soldiers some 150 meters away. He hurled grenades and sprayed automatic fire at the sentry, who panicked and ran away, allowing him free entry into the base. He fired his AK-47 and threw grenades into tents used by Israeli soldiers, killing five and wounding seven, but was finally shot and killed by the battalion cook who had been wounded. The shame brought about by the condemnation in the national press and army inquiries only reinforced many citizens negative opinion of Nahal. To add insult to injury the base name 'Gibor' meant 'Hero'.

I remember a return trip to Israel after the army and the El Al security check at Manchester Airport.

'Hebrew or English?' asked the security officer.

'Hebrew is fine' I replied with a heavy Manchester accent.

'How do you know Hebrew?'asked the officer.

'I served in the army, well sort of, I was in Nahal' I said.

The security officer smiled, 'Yes, I know what you mean, sort of' he replied.

I walked off with mixed emotions. I had been belittled for my army service but at least I had avoided a rigorous airport search.

There is hardly a book on Israel that does not bring in The Holocaust. The genocide of over six million Jews during The Second World War. There is no Jew who will ever forget. There are survivors and relatives of survivors who will never forgive. Riots in Israel followed the signing of a reparations agreement with Germany in September 1952. Many Israelis refused to travel on the trains and Mercedes buses given by the Germans. They labelled the reparations as blood money. To this day my father will not purchase German goods, be it a car or coffee machine. I once met, however, a non Jewish German couple in Jerusalem. Apologetic and embarrassed by their ancestors actions, they were genuinely proud and impressed by the state of Israel. As a Western Jew, I was educated on Nazi Europe, the Death Camps, Anne Frank. But half of the Israeli population are not European descendants. They too suffered in Arab countries. Throughout 1947 and 1948, Jews in Algeria, Egypt, Iraq, Libya, Morocco, Syria, and Yemen were persecuted, their property and belongings were confiscated, and they were subjected to severe anti-Jewish riots instigated by their governments. In Iraq, Zionism was made a capital crime. In Syria, anti-Jewish pogroms erupted in Aleppo and the government froze all Jewish bank accounts. In Egypt, bombs were detonated in the Jewish quarter, killing dozens. In Algeria, anti-Jewish decrees were swiftly instituted and in Yemen, bloody pogroms led to the death of nearly 100 Jews.

Of the almost one million Jewish refugees from Arab countries, between 1948 and 1972, around 200,000 found refuge in Europe and North America while the remainder were resettled in Israel - at great expense to the new State of Israel, and without any compensation from the Arab governments who had confiscated their possessions. The majority of the Jewish refugees left their homes penniless and destitute and with nothing more than the shirts on their backs. These Jews, however, had no desire to be repatriated in the Arab World and little is heard about them because they did not remain refugees for long. While most of these refugees understand that their suffering may not have been on the same huge scale of that in Nazi Europe, they still suffered. Many Jews were murdered and oppressed in once safe Arab countries. Many felt their stories were not heard in Israel, let alone in the diaspora.

Opponents of Israel say the state is Western guilt for the Holocaust, that without it the state would not have emerged. It probably would have, as, in addition to the Jews already living in Palestine, immigration began between around 1880 and 1900 with 35,000 Jews mainly from Russia. By 1940 the Jewish population had reached almost half a million.

Interestingly it is estimated that 50,000 Arabs immigrated to Palestine from neighbouring lands between 1919 and 1939 attracted by the improving agricultural conditions and growing job opportunities, most of them created by the Jews. While it is true the majority of Jews fled persecution be it from the Eastern European pogroms or The Nazis, many settled to satisfy their biblical beliefs in the Jews living in the Holy Land.

So why a section on the Holocaust and the purge of Jews in Arab lands in a chapter on the army? Because the State of Israel, The Israel Defence Force, is not simply an army to defend The State of Israel. It is the Jewish Defence Force. It was they who rescued the hostages from the Air France Entebbe hijacking in July 1976. Besides the 94 Israelis, they rescued 148 non Israeli passengers and 12 crew. Because from the Romans to the Crusaders to the Spanish Inquisition to the Russian pogroms to the Nazis there was nobody to protect or defend the Jews. With a few exceptions even the Jews didn't defend the Jews. The exception of Warsaw Ghetto Uprising where around seven hundred Jews from a population of around sixty thousand stood up and fought for the Jews. In August 1943, an uprising took place at the Treblinka extermination camp. Several German and Ukrainian guards were killed. The guards replied with machine-gun fire, and 1,500 inmates were killed, yet 70 inmates escaped.

In October 1943, an uprising took place at Sobibór extermination camp, The inmates covertly killed 11 German SS officers. The inmates had to then run for freedom under fire, with roughly 300 of the 600 inmates in the camp escaping alive. All but 50 to 70 of the inmates were killed in the surrounding minefields or recaptured and executed by the Germans. Some Jews were present in Partisan and resistance groups but as a whole they mostly walked to their deaths without a fight.

Now Israel was here as a safe haven should the unimaginable happen again and the Israeli army was here to protect that State and all Jews wherever they lived.

Chapter 4 Brothers in Arms

August 14th 1984


We came together, Little men, boys in green

Silliest sight, Craziest vision I've ever seen

We played together, Over the hills, through the sand

We all swore, We'd fight to the last man


We cried together, Tears of pain stained our uniforms

No escape, Even through crumbling walls

We laughed together, Laughed away the hate

Brothers with arms, Not quite Alexander the Great


We fought together, Enemies within and without

Searched for reasons to believe, Ways to dispel the doubts


We loved together, Made promises no intentions to keep

Sold our souls for a beer and a steak, Lied for just an hours sleep

we parted together, Still carrying the weights on our backs

Somehow we're stronger than ever, As we look back along the tracks.


The number one hit in the UK was 'Two Tribes' by Frankie goes to Hollywood. On this day in 1969 British troops were first deployed to Northern Ireland. The last execution took place in England in 1964 and in 1961 the Berlin Wall was erected.

My head hurt, but then all our heads hurt. The 5am alarm call shattered my drunken sleep and with eyes barely open I climbed over my girlfriend Ruth and fumbled for my clothes. Ruth called me back for a farewell kiss . I struggled back across the room to carry out my first order of the day. It wouldn't be the last for sure. There was no time for long good-byes or even a quick strong coffee. Dawn had broken. Our time was here. This was our call of duty. We had been given precise information on what to take with us on the first day. We knew we would be running half the night with all our bags and equipment so the less weight we took, the less we would have to carry. Everybody had their own advice but all were with one voice on one item, toilet paper. The girls waved off their brave men from the kibbutz bus stop. Within fifteen minutes we had arrived at Kiryat Shmona and were on our way to the army office in Tiberas.

Following some minor checks we were put into taxis (the only luxury we got from the army) and driven to the main induction centre, The Bakum, near Tel Aviv. The Bakum was where every soldier began his service. It was filled with young Israelis and older new immigrants all half frozen with terror and fear. Even at this early hour outside the gates was carnival like. Hundreds crowded the road outside as each of the young Israelis had brought their own entourage of family and friends. Throughout the Jewish world a boy becomes a man at thirteen. It is celebrated with family and friends and an overpriced dinner and dance. The new man receives expensive gifts and painful pats on the back in payment for singing, hopelessly out of tune, a couple of pages of the bible. With puberty a distant aspiration, the electric shaver either remains in the box for a few more years or is used as eyebrow trimmers. Meanwhile in Israel a boy becomes a man at The Bakum. The Israeli boy is brought to The Bakum by his father who hugs him with pride and a mother hugging her baby with fear. He makes his way through the gates with his bag filled with homemade food. Father offers a clenched fist, mother cries and his friends blow whistles and cheer the poor boy to manhood.

The phrase 'Helem Bakum', Shock Bakum, is most appropriate as the new recruits move from office to office in complete shock. We were greeted by a screaming officer, at least half our age, and shunted through several ludicrous medical tests. We entered the room in our underwear and T shirts. The doctor dragged himself up from behind his desk as we lined up ready for inspection. He clearly did not want to be there. I was not sure we did either. He moved along the line forcing his cold instrument into each of our ears, he then looked into our eyes and finally gazed with hopelessness into our mouths.

'All fit' he muttered 'All of you circumcised?' he questioned rhetorically. Nobody spoke.He finally smiled possibly comforted there wasn't a single foreskin amongst us.

'Beseder, culam tishim ve sheva' (OK, everybody ninety-seven').

Of course we all passed as fighting fit and were given a medical profile of ninety-seven (our circumcised penis depriving us of a perfect score).

Following the less than in depth medical we sat our Hebrew knowledge test. Here we were simply advised to write 'do not speak Hebrew' on the top of the page without answering any of the questions. The questions, interestingly, were questions on our actions during a war scenario. I wasn't sure how we would have answered the questions anyway just a couple of hours into our service. We all passed. Finally, after several hours of bouncing from office to office we were issued our papers. Finally we were sent to get our uniforms and miscellaneous equipment. We received the following:

A kit bag, Two towels (medium size), Three pairs of underwear, three white vests and five pairs of grey socks, three pair of army pants, shirts and one belt. One Beret, pair of boots. A bag full of miscellaneous equipment, one sweater, one winter jacket. While our clothing was all new, the rest of our equipment was all in need of serious repair. Our Casda (helmet) came without webbing, our gun magazines came with added rust. Our lime green berets showed we were new meat as did the red tags we pinned on our shirt lapels. We would have to walk fifty kilometres for a black beret, or, as I did, just walk part of the way and buy one from the army shop. We made sure that everything fitted, especially the boots. If anything was the wrong size or badly broken, it was immediately changed. Once ready and checked, you had to sign for the equipment. If something was broken or didn't fit, it wasn't possible to change it after signing for it. We sat on the wooden benches in a room not unlike a football changing room changing our civilian t shirts and shorts for the olive pants and shirts of the Israel Defence Force. I slipped my army ID card into my back pocket and my dog tag around my neck. Fuck, I was a soldier.

By late afternoon gone were our civies, our independence and our freedom. It wouldn't be long before we would lose our dignity too. We were now property of the army. A soldier attempting suicide could be charged with damaging army property. I was no longer Johnny Wallman, not even Yonatan Wallman. I was soldier number 1596030. The bus finally left The Bakum late in the afternoon. We headed for our new home at Mahane Shmonim, Base 80. Close to Tel Aviv and surrounded by huge eucalyptus trees, this base, as we would later find out, was not unlike every other army base. The only difference was the image of the green and white sickle and sword denoting a Nahal unit. The bus entered the main gate passing the sports field and basketball court. To the right the camp commanders room and office. Painted white stones formed the border of a small, quaint garden resembling a scene from Little House on the Prairie.

The bus halted at the junction where we were screamed off the bus towards our tents. There seemed little chance of a quiet night in with a takeaway and a bit of TV. We spent the entire evening and almost all of the night running from one side of the basketball court with our filled kit-bags and sometimes even our beds. It was a brutal introduction to the army. Our officer had followed us through our journey at The Bakum randomly barking orders. He was a sergeant and new immigrant also and barely a year into his army service. He appeared to have a serious chip on his shoulder and attempted to compensate by behaving overly aggressively. We understood the need for a firm hand but he took it too far. Perhaps we were in shock but he appeared overly sadistic especially when laughing as we carried our beds across the basketball court. The following morning he introduced us to the platoon commander but by that evening he was gone. I don't know if it was planned and his role was to simply 'introduce' us to the army, or, as rumour had it, he was replaced for over stepping the line with his previous nights treatment. For us it was simply the replacement of one arsehole for another.

I was a 'Chayal Boded' (Lone Soldier). We were mostly all lonely soldiers. This was a term given to soldiers who were in the country without their immediate family. There were probably around five thousand throughout the whole army. It did have its compensation's. We were allocated a special representative who looked after any issues we may have had. We received a slightly higher rate of pay than the average soldier and at certain Jewish festivals we received an extra gift. Soldiers departing for weekend or holiday leave were supposed to be released from the unit in time for them to reach their place of residence by noon, allowing them time to organise what they need for Shabbat or holidays. This never happened. A Chayal Boded whose parents lived overseas was eligible to receive a phone card. The card entitled the soldier to a certain number of minutes per month, in calls to any destination in the world. This was fine except for the fact you had to go through the army operator to make the call and she would listen in to the conversation. I was not privy to top secret information but even expressing a political opinion was not acceptable in the army. A Chayal Boded was entitled to one Yom Siddurim every month during their basic training. After basic training, one Yom Siddurim is granted every two months to take care of necessary errands. This too rarely happened. This was not deducted from annual leave or special leave days. Leave for personal errands was granted during weekdays, not on Fridays or on the eve of holidays, and with the approval of the soldier's Mefaked. That only happened once and that was at Moshave Sade when our officer, Yuval, was away. There were also times when the term 'Chayal Boded' in uniform at a falafel stall got you an extra discount. Sometimes we could use the cover of our title to get a day off army business to organise personal business, after all we had no family in the country to do this for us. Far from being a stigma, there was a great deal of respect amongst Israelis for the Chayal Boded.

Chapter 5 No More Heroes

August 15ᵗʰ 1984

Morning came too soon, much too soon. It was one thing waking at 5am on kibbutz with a leisurely stroll to the apple orchard, black coffee in hand, but 5am on an army base running around a toilet block was a lot more painful. We would become really quite well acquainted with that toilet block. We were marched to breakfast. The base looked even less appealing in daylight. We shuffled more than marched towards the dining room. The gravel pounded under our heavy, new boots. Our heads already thumped from the officers screams. We struggled to keep the rows of three formation much to the disdain of the officers.

The dining room was full except for one long table in the corner. The noise from 400 men was deafening. We were 'fresh meat'. We sat in silence at the almost bare table. Breakfast consisted of hard boiled eggs, olives, margarine, cheese, jam, bread and coffee. In the winter deisa, porridge, was added to the menu. It was very sweet and warming and was actually quite tasty. Eating porridge and camping in tents were two activities I always refused to entertain after the army. The coffee was barely warm, the white shelled eggs were brown once shelled and the freshness of the bread but a distant memory. We later discovered the reason for the brown eggs, they were boiled in the same pot as the coffee. Ravenous, we devoured this bounty more suited to a condemned man, but then that was what we were.

Our work day was set out in hideous routine although sometimes we took lunch at 1pm rather than at noon. First inspection was at 5am so we were woken by the last guard of the night at 4am. It would take us an hour to make it. At 4am the guard switched on the tent light and wished us a very good morning. He, in return, was greeted with a barrage of abuse and flying boots. We all fell back to sleep for forty five minutes before the sudden realisation a new day, same shit is upon us. The fifteen minutes before inspection were spent frantically running around and dressing whilst trying to force open our heavy eyelids. Of course at 5am, as the sergeant inspected his warriors, one soldier sneezes or blinks and we start one of many thirty second runs around the toilet block. We marched to breakfast and marched back, all before 6am. By 8am we have cleaned the tent, swept the tent and dusted the tent. By 9am the tent needs dusting again. You never win. Shaving was torture. With my baby like sensitive skin I preferred to soak my razor in warm water as I took a lengthy hot twenty minute shower. Strangely this is not possible in the army and instead I ripped open half my face as a cold razor pulled out my resistant facial hair. I was left with one of two results, neither acceptable to the officers, either a blood covered ripped face and neck or enough stubble to fill a pillow. Either way as the sergeant scrapes his piece of card across my damaged face I fail the shave test. My only hope is to join the queue in the next tent for the use of Jeremy's battery operated shaver.

Lunch was the main meal of the day. First course rotated between vegetable soup and minestrone soup although I maintain they were one of the same. Main course, almost always served with rice, were chicken wings. Once a week we did get battered fish which somehow tasted of chicken. The banquet would be complimented by a side salad usually consisting of a few lettuce leaves and a tomato. Dinner was a repeat of breakfast without the eggs. Much like the menu you receive on an airline, the description vastly plays up the actual meal. Chicken oriental noodles in a soy sauce served with winter vegetables turns out to be a pot noodle. After lunch we received an hours free time. This time we usually used valuably by sleeping or complaining. Those with the most talent managed to do both at the same time.

First task was to repair the equipment we had received at The Bakum. Magazine cases held together by rust, webbing on our helmets torn and ripped. If this was the equipment of the best army in the middle east I shuddered to think what the others had. Whatever our task, we were interrupted every half hour or so by the officers. A routine run around the toilet block. One of our few achievements was the development of our waterproof pack. The survival pack consisting of matches, a razor blade and shoe lace had to be waterproof. It was impossible. The pack encased in plastic and sealed with candle wax split open every time we hit the deck. Finally Andy placed the contents in an empty camera film canister. Sealed and waterproof. Success. Late in the day we were given our M16 weapons. Our weapons were our loved ones, our wives or girlfriends we were told. You went everywhere with your gun. If caught without your gun, punishment was severe but actually it rapidly became second nature to carry it everywhere. In fact, it so became second nature that after the army, when out shopping, you would automatically reach to your side to steady your imaginary gun.It didn't take long to feel naked without it. Of course everything came with strings attached or rather without this time. It took a 5km jog around the orchards of nearby Pardes Hannah for the right to put the straps on the guns. This was our first big run and gave the officers an opportunity to check out their soldiers. Todd, Jeff and Peter led from the front. Myself, Stuart, Moshe and Grandad Malcolm trailed a little behind. Kenny was lost amongst the orange trees..

Exhausted we returned to base and our beds. Each tent housed between twelve and fifteen soldiers. We carried out guard duty, for what is was worth as we had guns we had never used, had been given no training on how to use them and had no bullets in our magazines. Three soldiers guarded per one hour shift throughout the night and day. We were told that under no circumstances do you leave your post during 'Shmira' , guard duty. One soldier, desperate for the toilet but so afraid to leave his shift even pissed himself.

# Chapter 6 Heroes

August 17th 1984

We had only been soldiers for two days and already desperate for leave. All but two of the thirty soldiers in the platoon would be allowed home for the weekend. The selection process was called Mispar Mavet, number of death. Each soldier took a number and the officers would choose two random numbers. Whoever had chosen those numbers would stay back to guard the base. Every soldier wished the cruel hand of fate onto someone else. We were all desperate, already, for home. Nerves were frayed as the officer inspected us in our best uniforms. The air hung heavy as he passed us as fit for leave, except the two who would be remaining. As his lips uttered the two numbers I prayed to the god I had previously believed non existent he not call the number five, my number. Within seconds of his announcement two soldiers stood shattered in line as the remainder has already collected their bags and were almost at the front gate of the base.

Half the base stood at the bus stop jostling for prime position. It was basic mathematics, several hundred soldiers were never going to get on a bus with around seventy seats. Several buses arrived and filled before we got our chance. It was a huge juggling act getting on a bus with a large bag and a bulky M16 gun. It took practice, which we severely lacked. As we moved to the back of the bus, loud and jubilant, there wasn't a passenger who wasn't hit on the head by either a bag or a rifle butt. While we thought we were war heroes even after just two days service, our lapel stickers showed we were new soldiers. Everyone on the bus knew that but nobody said anything. They let us have our glory. It was a long journey home and within a short time of the bravado and loud outbursts we were asleep like babies. A few hours later we arrived in Kiryat Shmona sharing a beer at the local bar, still loud, still obnoxious and inappropriate. Again the locals let it go. They had been there themselves, they knew what we were in for later on.

Saturday morning and already it was a pleasure not to be woken by a screaming officer. I had visited The Fines, my kibbutz family, the previous evening. In Israel Sunday is a normal working day. Weekend in Israel is just one day, Saturday. Our one day weekend vanished in a haze of activity. By the time we had collected our clothes from the laundry, collected money from the office and bought any necessities for our return to base there was little of the day remaining. I loved the laundry service on the kibbutz, especially as a soldier. You deposited your dirty uniforms in the laundry on Friday evening and by Saturday lunch time they were returned cleaned and pressed. It was faster than mum. At the kibbutz shop I bought a dozen chocolate bars to take back to base. I knew they wouldn't last too long but enough to sustain me for a few days at least. We sat in the common room with the girls drinking coffee telling tales of our daring bravery. Obtaining that last chicken leg at lunch was the hell of war. The girls were incredibly supportive and attentive. They made us endless cups of coffee and even baked cakes. They listened to our bullshit with sincere interest. We watched The A Team on television. 'That's us' we cried. The girls just laughed for some unknown reason.

Girlfriend Ruth was still in Israel but coming to the end of her summer visit. She had been a member of the American class that studied there some years ago. Friday night I had miserably been unable to perform my boyfriend duties and waking in the middle of the night with the phrase 'I'm ready now' was not appreciated. Fortunately Saturday morning I was able to correct that. And Saturday afternoon. She was great and understanding. Returning home exhausted after active service I was never met with a 'to do list' like others in the garin. We didn't have to visit friends, go dancing, or cram weeks of boyfriend/girlfriend activity into four hours. She was perfectly happy sitting by my side as I struggled to lift my beer whilst curled on the bed watching television. She was genuinely understanding after I fell asleep during foreplay and accepted being woken in the early hours once my energy returned. We never discussed loving each other forever, I think we both knew that wasn't going to happen and were both fine with that. She was smart, school smart, at Cornell University, she was going to be a lawyer or something big like that, I was going to be a kibbutznik or a waiter or something like that. While she was in Israel I maintained my fidelity, it was a different matter when she was back in the States after Summer. We never discussed a future beyond my next weekend out. I think we both preferred it that way. Our group, with the exception of Jo and Susan, were living in Israel with our families abroad. Malcolm from Manchester, Moshe and Jeff from London, Yael Mexico, Todd, Peter, Kenny, Janet, Laura and Yaffa all from America. Sometimes we felt so alone but we tried hard to support one another. The garin was now our family.

Chapter 7 A Soldiers Song

August 21st 1984

Base 80 was our home for six months however we didn't bother ordering curtains and carpets. Our first six weeks before the arrival of our young Israeli colleagues were spent with a crash course in Hebrew alongside the rudiments of basic training. The army thoughtfully developed a hike for almost everything. For the honour of wearing our beret to the dubious perk of showering, we ran, then ran a lot more. Not that taking a shower was a particular treat. For obvious reasons cleanliness was extremely important. Our feet were constantly checked and serious failures resulted in punishment, usually extra guard duty or running on our dodgy feet. The shower block was horrendous. They had not been updated since the British Mandate and the trickle of water dripped freezing cold water. Forced showers were commonplace with us being checked for 'wetness'. We soon learned to just push our head underneath the water and liberally sprinkle water on our arms and legs.We were perpetually woken during the night and given three minutes to appear on parade in full uniform and with full kit. It was an impossibility without sleeping in full uniform. We would often spend the two or three weeks between home visits without showering or even removing our uniform. Once home, a brief whistle and your underwear and socks would skip voluntarily to the laundry.

Within the first month Stuart had gone. Having previously served in the U.S. Army he had the right to avoid active service. At first he opted to wave that exemption rule and serve with us. It became apparent that his tales of glory before the army were, if not fabricated, certainly exaggerated. He struggled just as we did. Things he should have known he didn't. Things he should have been able to do, he couldn't. We couldn't either but then we hadn't served several years in the American army. His lack of honesty caused friction between himself and others in the group. We were disappointed. The gossip sometimes became quite hurtful. It wasn't long before he became marginalised. It was suspected that while he had served in the American army, it had been as a cook or mechanic not as an infantry soldier. Really we didn't care, all we had wanted was honesty. We were all fresh and struggling, we could all pull through together but we had to trust each other. While he remained a member of the garin and on the kibbutz, he moved to non combat branch of the army. His weekend breaks differed from ours and we rarely saw him. He appeared to distance himself from the group. We spent a lot of time on our beds in our tents. The English speakers almost always spoke in their native tongue when away from the officers. English was banned and if caught a punishment of several turns around the toilet block was handed out. Looking back this was a sensible policy as there could be nothing more dangerous than a unit of soldiers advancing towards the enemy while all talking different languages. It was quite funny as we sat in our tents cleaning our equipment chatting in English until an officer approached where we would quickly switch to broken Hebrew. We learned pretty quickly some of the rules of the army. Number one rule was not to volunteer for anything. If you failed the volunteered chore you were punished by the officers, if you passed you were castigated by your comrades as a brown nose. If walking on the base you heard a cry of 'Chayal' or 'Soldier', the best policy was to ignore it and pretend you never heard. In almost all cases this was a shout from an officer with a request for a duty you would prefer not to carry out. Saluting was another big deal. You only salute an officer if he is wearing his beret and you got in as much trouble for an unwarranted salute as for a neglected one.

If learning Hebrew on kibbutz was tough, it was nothing compared to army studies. It wasn't easy sitting in on lessons on basic weaponry in a foreign language. There was the added hindrance of sleep deprivation. The lectures were constantly interrupted by the officer ordering a sleeping soldier to perform several circuits of the toilet block. In reality we learned very little save the skill of faking awareness. By the end of the six weeks, few, if any, could state the range of a rocket propelled gun. More unfortunately, nobody had obtained the phone number of the rather attractive Hebrew teacher.

It was strange being a soldier. Jews weren't really supposed to be soldiers. Yes we had the odd warrior in biblical times but not really over the past two thousand years. Jews were doctors and lawyers. The closest we ever got to war was either directing war movies or getting butchered in Europe. Maybe one of the reasons the Arabs failed in their attempted annihilation of the new Jewish state in 1948 was their miscalculation of the Jewish will to fight in a war. Since then we've done alright, actually pretty well as soldiers. From Moshe Dayan, the eye patch warrior to Yoni Netanyahu, the commander of the Entebbe rescue. As for me, five foot eight and nine stone heavy piss wet through I was hardly likely to strike fear through the ranks of the elite Syrian presidential guard. Reaction to my army service has been two similar sentences. Before the army I was met with 'What, you are joining the Israeli army?' while afterwards 'What, you were in the Israeli army?' Both contained the tone of incredulity.

The start of basic training for real brought more Israelis onto the base. Our platoon of all new immigrants was joined by two other platoons of young Israelis fresh out of high school. Most of our training would be done as a single platoon but we would carry out some exercises as a company. We were treated to a movie, The Great Escape. How little faith did our officers have in us? The girls still had not started their service but their fortnightly visits to base (except when we were out on exercise) were a godsend. The girls would bring with them treats from the kibbutz and any mail or packages from home. The two hour visit, besides being a welcome break from training, was a good opportunity to try and resolve any personal issues.

'Tirnut', 'basic training' was tedious. The actual training was fine but that took up only a fraction of our day. Most of out time was spent fixing our equipment or learning to follow orders, however benign. Our first inspection every morning always ended up with us running around the toilet block several times. We were supposed to stand rigidly to attention without anybody moving. Even if nobody so much as blinked, the officers would accuse us of breaking and order a circuit of the toilet block. We could spend time cleaning our equipment to perfection but still the officers would create a blemish and order us to repeat the task. Sometimes the sergeants would arrive at the inspection with dirt on their fingers and pass it on to our equipment causing us to fail. If we had four hours to clean, instead of giving us the four hours, we would be given one hour, get inspected, fail and repeat for another hour. This process would continue four times for four hours. All this was the build up to the commanders inspection where after three or four fails, we suddenly passed. While I understood the importance of following orders, it could save our lives later, treating us like school-kids proved counter-productive. Everything we did revolved around the prospect of us being involved in a war situation. If during a battle we had to march ten miles we knew we could because he had done fifty in training. If we had to go three nights with two hours sleep we could because in training we had gone three nights with no sleep.

Chemical warfare training was disturbing. We were taught the countless deadly chemicals owned by our neighbouring enemies, not least the Syrians. They had previously used nerve gas, mustard gas, sarin and countless other lethal chemicals.

Having used them on his own population, Assad, the Syrian Premier, was hardly likely to struggle with the morality of using them on a few Jews. We learned the symptoms of the gasses which included nausea, vomiting and death. We practised getting on our gas masks in the required time. We weren't actually issued with gas masks. This made a farce of our practising the task. During a real conflict by the time the masks arrived the chemical effects would have taken hold. I hoped that during a real war this oversight would be addressed by the commanders at the top. The training obstacle assault course was situated close to the main gate. Our weekly visit was not our finest day trip. With each visit our timing's improved a little. My struggle with climbing the rope continued. God I hated that thing. I was fine getting over the wall and crawling through the tunnels, and even climbing the rope wall, it was just wrapping my legs and gripping the single rope, I could just never grasp that method.We had struggled completing two circuits of the track on kibbutz and that was with a decent nights sleep and a full belly, this course was tough. There was also the banal on Base 80. The camp commanders house sat opposite the obstacle course. A wooden hut with a picket fence that looked more appropriate in an American western movie. Often a small detail of soldiers were seconded to sweep the surrounding area of leaves and litter, and to even whitewash the surrounding rocks. It was like a return to the British empire. The house looked completely out of place on the base. It wasn't the case but I imagined the camp commanders wife had demanded that if they move house that they literally move the house. Our equipment was beyond shoddy. The kazda (helmet) required webbing around it. A glue strong enough to secure the webbing has yet to be invented. All was fine until we began rolling down hills. The 'eford' (combat vest) was heavy before the pockets were filled with our gun magazines and full water container, which incidentally tasted of plastic even after its hundredth wash. Our army shirts were thick, heavy and brash. They retained the wet in the rain and heat in the summer sun. In their defence, they held up well when we bounced on the rocky slopes or crawled through the numerous nettles. In addition we had to maintain the units equipment such as the radio and the MAG gun. That was supposed to be a team effort.

I suppose the army is like a corporate business. The men at the top often dream up weird and wild initiatives that they believe 'a great idea'. The fact that in the army these men were once basic soldiers and once had the same mind set of us lowly privates, really they should have known better. One initiative, at weekends on base, we would hold a group discussion. For an hour, a precious hour we could have been sleeping, we would gather together as the officer would lead a group debate. The boundaries were no politics, no sex, no racism, no homophobic or disabled prejudices. Not much left really. All due respect to the officer but a twenty year old Israeli with plenty of army experience but no real experience of love nor life stands no chance against a bunch of older, more mature, well travelled, some married, experienced individuals. We would effortlessly redirect the talk to politics or sex from whatever the starting point. Our target was to get the debate abandoned in record time and give us a chance to return to our tents to sleep. I think the army only promoted this initiative to show the world the Israeli army was not simply a fighting tool, they were there to educate their soldiers, to show its humanity. It didn't work.

The officers hated us questioning their orders. Although the commands were never changed, sometimes it was just fun being pedantic.

'Why do we attack heavily fortified enemy posts in threes?' I asked the sergeant

'That's what we do in training' came his reply

'But it's suicide, we've got no chance in a real war' I continued 'Do we get air cover in a real conflict?'

'I hope so' came his reply

'And working on our kit, why not just give us two hours straight instead of four half hours and pretending each half hour that is the inspection?'

'Well, that is the army way, that is what we are taught.' replied the sergeant.

'And the radio codes, do the Arabs know our codes?' I pushed

'Of course they do' he replied with a huff

'so why use them, why say Perach (flower) for a killed soldier when they know we mean dead soldier and where the hell do you get flower as a code for a dead person. Surely a flower is a sign of life, of beauty not a sign of death.'

The officer was cornered now. 'I don't know,' he went on 'because the army does it that way'. Then he would have the last word and put me firmly in my place, 'because thank god the way we do it, however dumb it may seem, we haven't lost a war yet and we all know what would happen if we did lose a war'

I shut up then.

The girls had joined basic training on Mahane 80.Their training was every bit as rigorous as ours. Their tents were on the opposite side of the camp, a good distance from ours. We were not allowed to mix with them except on garin days when Rita would visit from Kfar Blum and we would spend a couple of hours picnicking and complaining. Most nights we were too tired and shattered to sneak across to the girls tents but we did visit sometimes.

Chapter 8 Blue Moon

October 1st 1984

Amongst my mail from England was my regular issue of the Manchester Evening News Football Pink. I had been a regular subscriber of the football newspaper every Saturday evening of the soccer season. The newspaper reported on the days matches, often games I had attended but had a very different view of how 'our boys' had performed. It was interesting how my surroundings when reading the paper had changed, from the plush Manchester Midland Hotel to a tent on an army base in the desert. No cappuccino and gateau here I was afraid. If City were to return to the first division then a drastic improvement was required on the average form of last season. I was delighted to receive packages from home, this one containing the promising news of Manchester City and the melted Mars Bar was a decent birthday reward. The mighty blues had started the season with four wins, two draws and two defeats, an average start. I had two spiritual homes, Israel and Maine Road, Manchester, home of my beloved Manchester City. The club was the idea of the daughter of Reverend Arthur Connell in the suburb of Gorton in 1879 as a method of providing entertainment for the male half of the parish. The name of Manchester City came into being at the start of the 1894/5 season. Transformed from Ardwick F.C. And accepted into the football league it was in 1904 that City won their first silverware beating Bolton in the F.A.Cup final. On December 1st 1906, 40,000 people saw City beat Manchester United 3-0 in the first ever Manchester derby. The start of a fierce rivalry that lasts until this day. On August 25th 1923 Manchester City played their first game at Maine Road beating Sheffield United 2-1. Horace Barnes had the honour of scoring the first ever goal at the new home. On March 11th 1941 the German airforce bombed Old Trafford, the home of Manchester United forcing the club to share the Maine Road ground. City charged United £5000 per annum for the privilege and years later in 1994 when City signed German star Uwe Rossler, chants and taunts from the City faithful claimed 'Uwe's grandad bombed Old Trafford' .

Both City and United were pretty much equally well supported in the community. In 1949 following the retirement of City legend goalkeeper Frank Swift, City Signed Bert Trautmann. Trautmann was a German prisoner of war paratrooper who had decided to remain in Britain after the war. Memories of the war were still fresh, many young men were still serving in the armed forces. There was a strong voice against having a German playing football for their team. While Trautmann became City's greatest ever keeper, playing the 1956 F.A.Cup final win against Birmingham City with a broken neck, many locals still could not accept a German in their team. They changed their allegiance to United. If local sympathy switched from blue to red over Trautmann, then national sympathy moved to United following the Munich air crash in February 1958 when, returning from a European game in Germany, the plane crashed in fog killing several United stars. Sadly it was forgotten by many City fans, when their sick taunts are displayed at derby matches, that also killed was City legend Frank Swift who was then a newspaper reporter covering the game.

In 1975 I was a thirteen year old football fan with no allegiance to any particular football team. I was invited to a City game with my friend Ian Wax and his father. I was hooked. I don't remember the game but I recall winning £10 for predicting the precise time of the first corner of the game. I continued attending the remainder of the games for the season. The following year I bought my first season ticket for Manchester City. As we sat in the Platt Lane Stand four nil was the popular chant as we dissected through our opponents like a knife through butter, often four nil. In February 1976 I attended Wembley to watch Barnes and a Tueart overhead kick, help city lift the League Cup in a two-one victory over Newcastle United. City finished a disappointing eighth in the league.

These were my glory days, City's glory days. Corrigan, Donachie, Doyle, Watson, Oakes, Barnes, Bell, Royle, Hartford, Tueart, Power, Marsh, Owen, Channon, did I mention Colin Bell? Heroes, my heroes. The following season City finished second in league, one point behind Liverpool. City were playing attractive entertaining football and it was great. And to add to the joy, United were distinctively average.

The joy never lasted long. Over the coming years heroes moved clubs or retired to be replaced by less than average players. Chairman Swales brought back manager Malcolm Allison. Fans were confused and dismayed by both the sale of firm City favourites and the purchases of new players, not least Steve Daley from Wolves for a staggering one and a half million pounds. Without improvement on the field Allison went, replaced by John Bond and more dubious signing's. While in Israel Year Course City reached the F.A Cup final drawing a thrilling match 1-1. Unfortunately the replay saw city lose an even more exciting game 3-2. Football hooliganism was rife in England and while there was no crowd trouble at Wembley, there was certainly trouble with us watching the game in Jerusalem. By participating on a Jewish course, certain Jewish traditions were expected to be observed. One of these was the observance of the Sabbath. We were not permitted to watch television on a Saturday. This provided us with a dilemma on how to watch the game in the common room. Several of us decided to barricade ourselves in the room by putting chairs and tables up against the doors. Shortly after the initial kick off group leaders launched an offensive banging on the doors and forcing their entry. The television was switched off and we were reprimanded. These Yanks had no understanding of the importance of 'Soccer' as they called it.

On my return from my year in Israel I had passed my driving test and attended City matches with Simon. It took a perverse dedication to stand in The Kippax Stand on a freezing, wet and miserable January day watching your beloved team struggle to put together three passes. City were awful. Mid table in 1981/2 became relegation the following season. City were relegated with Brighton who hammered City 4-0 out of the F.A.Cup. May 14th 1983, 42,000 fans crammed into Maine Road, including myself and Simon. City needed a draw to stay up while Luton, their opponents required a win to remain in Division One. With four minutes from safety a deflected shot from Luton's Raddy Antic slipped past City keeper Alex Williams. City were down and tears rolled down my face, and Simon's as Luton manager David Pleat performed his famous

Jig on the Maine Road pitch. I left City for Israel at this point. I wouldn't be present physically but in spirit I was city till I die. As luck would have it my birthday fell on Jewish New Year leaving us free from training for two days. With cards and gifts somewhat in on the ground Jeremy did present me with a Mars Bar and as a group we licked the wrapper. It was quiet around the base. There was none of the usual hustle around the base. The few religious soldiers left for prayer while the rest of us relaxed on our beds. It was a good opportunity to write home, a better opportunity to grab some extra sleep. I took out a letter home I had started earlier and continued it. I played down the uncomfortable conditions, lack of food and deprivation of sleep. There was no point in upsetting them more than necessary. With the kitchen closed we ate battle rations, even worse than the gruel we usually received. Kosher spam in a tin tasted no better than the real thing.

October 6th 1984 Turn, Turn, Turn

The fast day, Yom Kippur marks the day when Jews fast for a day in order to repent their sins. Sins that of course we would likely repeat the following year. It is particularly poignant in the army as in 1973 the armies of Egypt, Syria, Jordan and Iraq launched a surprise war bringing Israel close to the brink. The Yom Kippur War started with a surprise Arab attack on Israel on Saturday 6th October 1973. Egyptian and Syrian military forces launched an attack knowing that the military of Israel would be participating in the religious celebrations associated with Yom Kippur. Therefore, their guard would temporarily be dropped. On the Golan Heights alone, 150 Israeli tanks faced 1,400 Syria tanks and in the Suez region just 500 Israeli soldiers faced 80,000 Egyptian soldiers. Other Arab nations

aided the Egyptians and Syrians. Iraq transferred a squadron of
Hunter jet fighter planes to Egypt a few months before the war
began. Iraqi MIG fighters were used against the Israelis in the
Golan Heights along with 18,000 Iraqi soldiers. Saudi Arabia
and Kuwait effectively financed the war from the Arabs side.
Saudi troops, approximately 3,000 men, also fought in the war.
Libya provided Egypt with Mirage fighters and in the years
1971 to 1973, Libya bankrolled Egypt's military
modernisation to the tune of $1 billion which was used to
purchase modern Russian weapons. Other Arab nations that
helped the Egyptians and Syrians included Tunisia, Sudan and
Morocco. Jordan also sent two armoured brigades and three
artillery units to support the Syrians, but their participation in
the war was not done with vast enthusiasm. Cuba sent
approximately 4,000 troops, including tank and helicopter
crews to Syria, and engaged in combat operations against the
IDF. 20 North Korean pilots and 19 non-combat personnel
were sent to Egypt. The unit had four to six encounters with
the Israelis from August through the end of the war.

Facing such an attack, the Israeli forces were initially swiftly
overwhelmed. Within two days, the Egyptians had crossed the
Suez Canal and moved up to fifteen miles inland of the most
advanced Israeli troops in the Sinai. Syrian troops advanced by
the same distance into the strategic Golan Heights in north
Israel. By the end of October 7th, the military signs were
ominous for Israel. However, on October 8th, Israeli forces,
bolstered by called-up reserves, counterattacked in the Sinai.
They pushed back the Egyptian military and crossed the Suez
Canal south of Ismailia. Here, the Israelis used the Suez-Cairo
road to advance towards the Egyptian capital, Cairo, and got to
within sixty miles of it. The Israelis experienced similar
success in the Golan Heights where the Syrian forces were

pushed back and Israel recaptured lost land. Using the main road from Tiberias to Damascus, the Israelis got to within thirty miles of the Syrian capital. Syria ignored the Geneva Conventions and many Israeli prisoners of war were tortured or killed. Advancing Israeli forces, recapturing land taken by the Syrians early in the war, came across the bodies of 28 Israeli soldiers who had been blindfolded with their hands bound and executed. In December 1973 Syrian Defence Minister stated that he had awarded one soldier the Medal of the Republic for killing 28 Israeli prisoners with an axe, decapitating three of them and eating the flesh of one of his victims. The Syrians employed brutal interrogation techniques utilising electric shocks to the genitals. A number of Israeli soldiers taken prisoner on Mount Hermon were executed. Near the village of Hushniye, the Syrians captured 11 administrative personnel from the Golan Heights Force, all of whom were later found dead, blindfolded and with their hands tied behind their backs. Syria would not release the names of prisoners it was holding to the International Committee of the Red Cross and in fact, did not even acknowledge holding any prisoners despite the fact they were publicly exhibited by the Syrians for television crews. Historian Aryeh Yitzhaki estimated that the Egyptians killed about 200 Israeli soldiers who had surrendered.

Israel suffered between over 2,500 casualties and an additional 8,500 soldiers were wounded. Arab casualties were known to be much higher than Israel's, though exact figures are difficult to ascertain as Egypt and Syria never disclosed official figures. The casualty estimate is between 8,000 and 18,500 Egyptian and Syrians killed. On the night of September 25, before the war, King Hussein of Jordan secretly flew to Tel Aviv to warn Israeli Prime Minister Golda Meir of an impending Syrian attack. 'Are they going to war without the Egyptians? asked Mrs. Meir. The king said he didn't think so. 'I think Egypt would cooperate.' This warning was ignored. Throughout September, Israel received a dozen warnings of war from well placed sources. However, Mossad Director-General Zvi Zamir continued to insist that war was not an Arab option, even after Hussein's warning. The war was won and the country saved. But yet again, following a victory, many Israelis struggled with the after effects. In 1967, following the capture of Jerusalem and The West Bank, one major question from the Israeli on the street was 'What do we do with all these Palestinian Arabs?' A million Arabs that had previously lived under the control of Jordan now had the Israel as their guardian. Many soldiers felt that what had began as a war for survival became a war of occupation. Many Arabs were thrown out of their homes and exiled to Jordan. Israeli soldiers watched mothers carry their children as refugees. They remembered themselves being carried by their own mothers exiled by The Nazis. They felt deeply uncomfortable. Of course the Palestinian Arabs were not being marched to death camps but they were losing their homes. Before the War of independence in 1948 and The Six Day War of 1967, Arab leaders especially in Egypt, Syria and the Mufti of Jerusalem, urged Palestinian residents to leave their homes while the Jews were wiped out. They told them to be ready to return after a great Arab victory. There were also Israeli army units that forcefully emptied Arab villages of their residents. There were faults and transgressions on both sides. Now in 1973 the questions were directed to the government, 'Why did you ignore the warnings? ' and to the intelligence service, supposedly the best in the world 'Why didn't you know?'

Chapter 9 Teach Your Children Well

October 13th 1984

On base it was another rest day and an opportunity to tune into the BBC World Service to gather the football results. City had now pulled themselves together earning a draw at Carlisle following four consecutive victories. As the religious departed again for prayers we remained in our tents to write home or sleep. We saw nothing of the officers, no inspections, no running around the toilet block. Joy. I was enjoying these festivals. Back in England I had attended synagogue during the festivals as a mark of respect to my parents and it was a useful opportunity to catch up with old school friends. Here in Israel, in the army, away from that, and with a chance for a couple of hours extra sleep, it was a no- brainer. Over the Jewish New Year period, countless festivals spread over a month, we were showered with gifts. From the army we received a photograph book of early nineteenth century settlements and settlers. A more thrilling gift I am yet to receive. Of more use was the towel we received as an extra gift for being a 'Lone Soldier'. The most poignant gift was the small shoe box. Written in blue marker 'To a brave soldier'. The box was filled to overflowing with chocolate, sweets, soap, shampoo and even a pair of bootlaces. Also inside, a handwritten note from a schoolkid in Afula.

'Dear Soldier, My name is Yehuda, I am ten years old. I live in Afula with my family and cat. My dad goes to the army and is sad when he goes. If you are sad I hope you get happy with my gift. When I am big I will be a hero soldier like my dad and you. Thank you for protecting us.'

I felt a fraud. I was no hero, not yet anyway, not nearly. I wasn't going to write to Yehuda and contradict him. I wrote back.

'Dear Yehuda, Thank you so much for your gift. The candy really cheered me up. My name is Yoni, I came from England to live here. I will always protect you.'

The sad fact was that in a few years Yehuda will be sat on a base himself opening a shoe box from a different Yehuda. This shit was never going to end.

With the closing of the festival we were ordered to collect our kit bags and equipment. We were off camping. Givat Olga was hell. The five hour trek through farmland and orchards was not helped by carrying Kenny by stretcher the majority of the way. His so called injury renewed the memories of our last night before the army on kibbutz. He had shown his true colours at the river side and now again in some muddy field on the way to Givat Olga. He was lazy and had no qualms about dumping his heavy over weight body onto a stretcher for his 'friends' to carry. Over the next few days resentment towards him grew, from those in our garin and others. Kenny would be the second member of the garin to opt out of a combat unit. He, unlike Stuart, left the kibbutz. We never saw him again.

I never realised a country so small could have so many uninviting areas. Givat Olga was situated around forty kilometres north of Tel Aviv on the coast. It was a neighbourhood of Hadera. Hadera was home to Israel's first paper mill, Israel's largest power plant and the world's largest desalination plant. According to one website some years later 'the scenic part of Hadera includes Givat Olga, which is both the name of Hadera's largest neighbourhood as well as Hadera's beach. The beach is an inviting stretch of sandy beach, followed by pleasant and romantic coves as you head south of the main beach'. Givat Olga was named after Olga Hankin, wife of Yehoshua Hankin who purchased the land where Hadera was founded. As I remember it the sands were not so golden and the prominent feature of the landscape was the Hadera power station a little further up the coast. There were no topless sunbathers on this beach, just ropes, tents and a group of soldiers running along the shoreline.

Our training still comprised mainly of running and near starvation. It didn't help that most of the food was stolen, presumably by the locals, during the night. We awoke to find breakfast had been cancelled due to the loss of the food. This was our first introduction to battle rations. Tins of Kosher Spam, Tuna, chocolate spread and bread so stale it was minutes from its expiry date. We filled our mess tins with the meagre rations best we could. Like the rush for the extra chicken leg on the base, here the same fight for a tin of compressed mush. The army issue cutlery was useless and there was no time to wash our hands. How we didn't all come down with severe food poisoning was a miracle. We ate like savages, starving savages our dirty fingers serving as a knife, fork and spoon. Olga was our first real training. Army training differed greatly from civilian training. In civilian life the individual is shown what to do, explained how to carry out the task and nurtured for a reasonable time until they have grasped the concept.In the army the process is much more simple. An officer explains in ten or less words what he wants doing and the soldiers attempt to carry out the task. If you are fortunate enough to grasp the concept fine, if not then the army believes you will eventually and leaves you to learn it yourself. How more recruits are not killed or injured on the rifle range or during grenade practice is amazing.

Yuval pulled out his first three victims from the group, myself one of the unfortunate.'You see that mound over there, attack it' he instructed pointing at a small clump of earth around two hundred metres away. Those were the instructions. No demonstration, no detailed plan. Instinct and common sense told us to hit the ground and start crawling. We didn't see the nettles on the ground until it was too late. In unison we let out a yelp of pain interpreted by Yuval as a battle cry. I think he was impressed. Using our knowledge of several war films the three of us split up several metres from the mound. One carried on forward, one circled to the left, the other to the right. The nettle scars were nothing compared to what would probably happen in a real battle where the bunker was defended by heavy artillery. Once we had taken our turn we sat up on the nearby rocks and watched our comrades in action. Watching others carry out the operation showed how flawed the strategy really was..it was hard to believe this was a real practise for a warfare operation, more like an excuse for Yuval to watch us squirm through nettles.

Chapter 10 Once I Was

October 18th 1984

With Olga behind us and still bearing the scars we were posted on our first outside guard duty. Petech Tikva was a small town about ten kilometres east of Tel Aviv. It was founded in 1878 by mainly Orthodox Jews with a population growing to around 200,000. During the Sinai and Palestine Campaign of World War I, Petah Tikva served as a refugee town for residents of Tel Aviv and Jaffa, following their exile by the Ottoman authorities due to their refusal to serve the Ottoman army to fight the invading British forces. The town suffered heavily as it lay between the Ottoman and British fronts during the war.

Petah Tikva became the school for thousands of pioneer workers, who studied the craft of farming there before they ventured out to establish dozens of settlements in all parts of the country. The agricultural schools were still active. Petah Tikva was also the birthplace of the Labour Zionist Movement, inspired and encouraged by the writings of A. D. Gordon who lived in the town. The first recorded Arab attack on Jews in Palestine took place in Petah Tikva in 1886. Petah Tikva was also the scene of Arab rioting in May 1921, which left four Jews dead.In the early 1920s, industry began to develop in the Petah Tikva region. In 1921, Petah Tikva was given the status of a local council by the British authorities, and in 1937 it was recognised as a city. Nothing dramatic had happened there in fifty years. We were deployed there to patrol the local park called Afek and the local streets for the final festival of the month. It was more a show to reassure locals than an actual meaningful exercise. We were housed overnight in the local police station sleeping on mattresses on the floor and fed battle rations. On the eastern side of the city is a huge Park Afek with an ancient medieval crusaders fortress still standing. Myself and Peter paired off for patrol of the park. We would spend five hours watching the locals enjoy their picnics, our reward being a tin of bully beef and stale crackers back at the station later. With the October sun beating down, we struggled at times with our heavy equipment. The park was full of picnickers and children playing football or frisbee. As we patrolled, the tempting smell of the barbecues emanated from every corner of the park. We hovered towards many to a total lack of subtlety. It was quite a while until we were invited over by one family. 'It is basar lavan (pork)' we were warned before tucking in. We laughed. As if eating forbidden non kosher meat would stop us. As if we would reject a pita bread filled with a juicy steak and salad in favour of a tin of army corned beef. Following our mains, now filled with confidence, we ambled towards another family for desert and completed our experience with a glass of wine and cheese from a French couple. The only major drama was when an elderly man collapsed through heat stroke. If this was practice for future street patrols, it was pretty much ineffective as the only hazards we had to deal with were the smoke off the barbecues and low flying frisbees. For Peter however the day ended in disaster when his knee gave way on a later patrol. A visit to the hospital diagnosed water on the knee forcing him to lower his army medical profile. Peter was the latest garin member that left the company later joining up with the girls.

It didn't take us long to figure out ways of avoiding particular tasks either on base or out in the field. Often the busiest man on the camp was the medic. At any one time up to a third of the combat soldiers could be 'out of action' due to one illness or another. Some were genuine. If you are running up and down hills with a full pack in burning heat there is a possibility of injuring a limb but many were a wheeze. These medics were battled hardened soldiers and a poorly finger didn't cut it for exemption of training when these guys have treated soldiers with blown off limbs in battle. Dehydration was the biggest issue and officers were beyond diligent. We were constantly warned about our water canteens and ordered to drink all the time. Diarrhoea was the illness of choice. No officer wanted to check the validity of the complaint and if they did you just led them to the communal hole in the ground, dodged the flies where there was no way to prove your shit from that of everybody else. Diarrhoea exempted you from kitchen duty for three days. You couldn't do guard duty because you may have gotten caught short and had to leave your post and obviously couldn't do training. Nobody wanted to crawl through the shit trail of the soldier in front of him. A 'Petor' ( sick note) gave you two or three days rest. It was useful but had to be used with thought. Too many too often and you risk pissing off your hard working colleagues, and the officers. Each task earned a reward, especially the hikes and forced marches. You hiked for the beret, the gun strap, home leave and everything else. Those who avoided the task had not earned that reward yet still either received the strap the gun or bought the beret in the army store. From the outside it appeared grossly unfair that the slackers prospered. From the inside the odd skive was looked upon as a clever ruse and congratulated. More than the odd skive and the offender was often castigated by the others. The trick was to find the balance.

Chapter 11 Drive my Car

November 8th 1984

For anybody with a poor record of exam results they could have done a lot worse than an army course. You never failed. Several of the platoon spent a week on an armoured personnel carrier (nagmash) course at a base at Revikim in the Negev desert. Again the army excelled at finding a place so desolate and bleak. I had no burning ambition to drive a Nagmash. However it seemed like a hoot, an experience. It was actually a lot of fun. Our first task on arriving on base was to erect our two man tents. Like a rash I ended up with Moshe again. From one kibbutz to another and then to the army, like some sorry wife, Moshe was there by my side. Firstly we had to dig a large hole half the height of the tent. Apparently this was to disguise the tent. I struggled with this army logic. Why bury half the tent? Surely you bury all of it or none. The top half of our temporary home was still visible for miles. In addition we were miles from civilization. I counted three scorpions and one snake as we dug the hole. I feared there would be more than just myself and Moshe in the tent that night.

Myself, Danny and Ian shared one vehicle. We took turns in driving up and down the small mounds of sand built for the challenge. The instructors were incredibly relaxed and appeared to enjoy the bumps. There were no drills or inspections and when we weren't driving we were free to relax with the local wildlife in our tents. First task of the morning was to empty our boots of scorpions. We were instructed to fold our socks over the top of our boots to stop the scorpions from climbing inside but clearly it didn't work. The remainder of the day was occupied driving the vehicles for just a couple of hours and relaxing in our tents. We all completed the course with a concussion, certificate but more importantly a weekend pass home. Ian was also from Manchester. He was two or three years younger than myself. We hadn't known each other in England. It turned out that for a few months Les, his father, and my father had served together in the British army during the Second World War. I think our parents found this more fascinating than we did. Les submitted a photograph of myself and Ian together in uniform to the local Jewish Newspaper, The Jewish Telegraph, where we achieved our fifteen minutes of fame.

Chapter 12 No Other Country

November 9th 1984

Hitchhiking was commonplace amongst soldiers. Although we did receive subsidised bus travel there were many motorists willing to help out soldiers by giving them rides. Most had been soldiers, tired, poor and desperate to get home themselves. There had been rare occurrences of soldiers being kidnapped or killed by terrorists, and soldiers were told not to hitch but they continued to do so. This was my first time and after a stuttering start I think I did pretty well actually beating the bus to Avigdor. This was even more of an achievement as I had waited almost an hour for a second car to stop as I had turned down the first lift. The driver had told me his destination and I hadn't realised that would take me through my required destination.

This was my first visit since joining up and the first time Stella and Ossi saw me in uniform. I felt incredibly proud and excited. I had family and friends in Israel. There were many people I loved and respected. Whenever I turned up on their doorstep in uniform I felt excited but this was different. I knocked on the door and Stella opened it with her usual gusto. Her eyes filled with tears of pride as she saw her Yonatan in the uniform of the Israeli army. Her hug took the wind out of me. It was her I was defending. I was looking forward to a decent meal, a hot shower and a bed with sheets. The problem at Stella's was the tendency to spend half the night chatting. Fortunately Stella understood how tired I was. For the first time ever at her house I was in bed and fast asleep before midnight.

Stella and Ossi lived on Moshav Avigdor near Ashkelon. Avigdor is a small Moshav (similar to a kibbutz) in southern Israel. It is located south of Kiryat Malakhi and 20 km north east of Ashkelon. Its population was around seven hundred. It was founded in 1950 by veterans of the British Army and was initially named Yael, the initials of Hebrew Units for Transportation, the unit that the veterans belonged to during the war. The population were partly agriculturist, their main occupation dairy farming, turkeys, chicken and various field crops and partly free profession (lawyer, accountant, engineer, etc.) The peace and quiet was often disturbed by the roar of the fighter jets from the nearby airforce base. I had first met the couple four years earlier when staying during my year course programme. Since then I had visited often. To me they were Israel. It is possible to write an entire book on both Stella and Ossi.

If Friday night had been early to bed, Saturday night was a return to form. We had relaxed, and talked all day but there was always room for another Stella story.

'Did I tell you about the Ugandan minister?' Stella had asked. I should have answered 'yes' thus prompting an end to our all night talk and a trip to my rarely visited single bed but I was far too interested and intrigued to miss this story. I sat back in my armchair and shuffled into a more comfortable position.

I had met Stella in 1980, through a friend. I stayed with her and her husband, Ossi, for a month. Admittedly I was 17 then and highly impressionable. Now, a little older, wiser and cynical, yet her awe still commanded my highest respect, love and regard. I knew she was born on April 24 but never found out what year, though I suspected around 1925. I could only apologise if falsely accusing her of old age. But that was the fantastic thing about her. For a woman in mature phase of life, she had an attitude towards life that would put a twenty year-old to shame.

Stella was born and raised in London. Given the choice of being the pampered wife of the head of Marks and Spencer, or risking malaria in the swamps of some far flung country, she chose the latter. I struggled to understand spurning a proposal of marriage to a wealthy business tycoon but understood the call of Israel. As we age, as the sunsets seem to come that much quicker, we look back at our achievements (or lack of). Maybe we can't dine on our memories, maybe they don't pay the bills, but they show us that just maybe we did serve some purpose here on this lonely planet.

'No, I would have remembered the ambassador story' I replied.

'Oh, it was just after the 1973 war. We had excellent relations with Uganda, then Idi Amin came to power' she continued. Her blue eyes stared as her hand fidgeted for her cigarettes. She displayed a momentary frustration at having misplaced them. I looked back into Stella's eyes. I saw her youth, her energy and felt a little ashamed at my own lethargy. I took out two cigarettes from my packet and handed her one.

'We should cut down,' she quipped.

Balancing the cigarette on her lip, she continued. 'So the foreign minister called me and explained that the Ugandan defence minister was due to visit the base just down the road.' She pointed towards the base, using her outstretched arm to light the Europa mild filter I had given her. 'The army wanted somewhere close to bring the minister for half an hour, for cold drinks before he inspected the troops. Well, I was asked and happily agreed.'

Without warning she stood, her ash falling on to her crumpled skirt. She walked to the bookcase behind the now vacant chair. The room was filled with books, wall to wall, the small house was filled with words. That is the best way I could describe her home. A house filled with words of love, humour, education, thought. I watched her walk to one bookcase and pull a leather folder case from the bottom shelf. She brought it to me, placing history in my hand.

Then matter of fact, as she related the story of a major part of the country's history, she walked to the kitchen to prepare yet another cup of tea. She talked from the kitchen as I hooked on her every word. Her voice raised as the kettle whistled and the spoon stirred the sweet tea.

'Anyway, the minister, surrounded by guards and officials, arrived at our farm here and we sat outside drinking lemonade and chatted. Well two hours later we were still chatting, the officials anxious to move on, the minister enjoying himself, the soldiers on the base standing ready for inspection in the burning heat. As they were leaving the minister shook my hand and passed this case to me.' I looked at the brown leather case. Embossed in the corner the words,

*Ministry Of Defence, Uganda.*

It felt so smooth, so powerful. I saw her smile as I looked up. I loved her stories and understood how she loved telling them. She talked of major figures of the political world as most would talk of their neighbours. There was no snobbery, no name-dropping, she knew many of them, knew them well and no big deal. I admired her modesty.

'Then he asked me if it was possible for his eldest child to stay on the farm for a few weeks, that he and his family would visit for a few days, his son would stay and experience life here. Really I couldn't say no. How can you refuse a minister of a foreign nation?' Her eyebrows raised. I wasn't sure if the question warranted an answer or was purely rhetorical. I smiled, that being the most appropriate action. My tea, by now, was only warm, my desire for another cigarette beginning to bite. Stella returned to her seat, collecting the folder as she passed me. I felt relief as she took it, like I had been relieved of guarding something precious.

'So, the next summer, all the family arrived and somehow, we all managed to squeeze into this matchbox.' We laughed together. I remembered my first visit. The home was about an hour's bus ride from the Jerusalem. My instructions were to get off the bus and walk up the road for around 500 yards. Stella's house was on the left after the main offices. Some of the houses I passed were huge, three story brick houses built on stone stilts. Stella's by contrast was a small wooden house probably the size of one of the rooms in the big houses. There was a small decked porch overlooking the now disused cowshed and the front lawn. Flowers of every colour, their beauty unrivalled, surrounded the neatly mowed lawn. Stella was particularly proud of the four trees in the garden, explaining that if one took a photograph at a certain angle, it could appear as if it had been taken in a forest. I soon discovered that size is not everything and all I needed was in Stella's small house while nothing needed could be found in the big houses.The clock had passed 2am as Stella continued her story. ' They had a fantastic time, but as they left, the minister took me to the side. He knew I was in touch with the Prime Minister here, he knew we were friends.'

'You knew the Prime Minister?' I asked, impressed and shocked

'Of course, and I used to baby-sit our once foreign minister' she replied. She seemed shocked that I was so impressed, as if I was the only person who never knew, as if anybody should be surprised.

'Anyway, he told me to talk to the Prime Minister and tell her to cancel their order to buy fighter jets. He told me there was a new man emerging, Idi Amin, and that he would not continue the good relations. The minister hugged me saying this would probably be the last time we would ever see him'.

I sat spellbound in his chair watching the emotion rise within Stella. I could see how hard it was for her to recount the story, but I guessed she needed to tell.

'I did as he asked but nobody listened' she went on, her deep blue eyes filling. I had never seen her upset and felt uneasy. I saw her as a rock, someone who had been through the refugee camps of Europe, four wars and three husbands. I saw how she cared, how after so much history, this event could still cause so much pain. But this was typical of Stella, she was there for the 'little man', the underdog.

'Idi Amin came to power, we were never paid for the planes and one day I read in the newspaper that the minister had been killed in a road accident.'

I looked to the roof for divine intervention but there was none coming. I sat silent not knowing what to say. Finally, after a long silence, Stella helped me.

'Well, it's late, we'll talk tomorrow'.

I retreated my bedroom. I barely slept.

Next morning I still had the Ugandan minister on my mind but clearly Stella hadn't. She set about milling around as Ossi prepared breakfast. The radio news emanated from Stella's bedroom. I heard the occasional outburst as she commented on each news feature. Ossi, who had already eaten, called us to the table while he excused himself. He would perform his daily ritual of walking the short distance to the local shop for milk, bread, a newspaper and 'her bloody cigarettes' before collecting the mail on the way back. The journey should have taken less than ten minutes, but Ossi would be gone nearly an hour. He always was. He would take his time and stop to talk to all those he met. If the truth were known, he was a secret gossip. Unfortunately, Stella, already knew the news he invariably brought back. She, not wanting to steal his thunder, would pretend to be shocked making out this was the first she had heard of it.

Stella buttered herself some toast as I sipped my coffee. We talked about the news and about our lives. I felt perfectly comfortable and relaxed. We brought our drinks into the front room and I passed Stella a cigarette.

'I must stop smoking all yours,' She said

I laughed, replying, 'It's ok, I've plenty'.

Ossi returned with his provisions placing the carrier bag on the kitchen table. Scanning through the bundle of letters, he read out their origins. 'Bill, bill, bill, France.' He turned the France letter over to search a return address.

'Whom do we know in France?' he asked Stella

'De Gaulle.' replied Stella, smiling.

Ossi handed her the letter and opened the remaining bills. Stella's face changed to shock as she pulled open the seal and a tiny note fell to the floor. Being the perfect gentleman, I picked up the folded note returning it to Stella. It had been folded at least half a dozen times, taking Stella a few seconds to unfold and read. In silence she handed it to me who instinctively read it aloud.

> *'I don't know if you remember me. I am the wife of the minister who visited you many years ago. He died suspiciously and now I need to get out of Uganda. Can you help please?'*

The room was deadly silent. Somehow the note had been smuggled out and posted in France.

Stella broke the silence.' There is no date on it, could have been written years ago, lost and just posted, besides I don't know anybody in the government now.' She became angry at her impotency. She had received a cry for help and was unable to do anything about it. But she couldn't simply do anything. She paced the room, like she was looking for an answer there, looking at books, calculating dates of events.

'Amin has been gone for years, they must have visited twenty years ago, and how did she get my address. Who smuggled it out and when?' Stella repeated the questions over and over; neither Ossi nor myself could come up with any answers.

Finally, with much of the day having been lost in a sea of confusion, Stella decided to call the Ministry of Defence. By this time she had the photographs of the family strewn on the table. I saw three people standing next to Stella, the cowshed in the background. All four smiled, only the minister knowing the future would not provide smiles, not for them anyway. I wondered if the minister knew at the time how imminent his demise was, that within a few months of the photo he would be dead. Stella dialled the number, her fingers shaking. I had never seen her nervous before. She lit yet another cigarette as she waited for an answer.

'Hello, Defence Ministry?' she asked before relating the tale of the Ugandan family to the receptionist. With her nervousness, Stella missed parts out having to recall them later in the story. I knew the story but still found it difficult to understand it as Stella talked. He pitied the poor girl on the reception trying to figure out what this old dear was twittering on at. The girl must have asked their name as Stella began spelling their surname, letter by letter. There was a brief silence then she turned white, again her eyes filling as she thanked the receptionist and hung up the phone. Stella turned to the silent Ossi and myself shaking her head.

'They keep records, as best they can, of political dissidents connected with this country. It is recorded that the husband died in a car crash, as we knew. The wife and son died in a house fire over three years ago.' She said

'So how did the note take three years to arrive?' asked the practical Ossi. Stella didn't answer. She didn't have one and wanted to close the chapter before her anger took over. We realised this and said no more. We looked at the bookshelf where the bag was kept and though out of sight, we could feel it burn into our hearts.

There appeared nothing remarkable about Ossi. His stature not the least bit imposing, his voice quiet and his tone not at all forceful. Often he would take himself away from his armchair into the kitchen where he would spend hours alone completing German puzzle books. On initial appearance he was not the kind of man you would think of inspiring.

I first met Ossi on Moshav Avigdor in 1980. He stood next to his wife Stella, who was considerably larger in both stature and personality. Perhaps that was part of Ossi's image problem, the fact that Stella, so much more overpowering, over shadowed Ossi. But Ossi had a huge personality, a fascinating history and a courage he simply preferred to keep to himself.

Much of Ossi's life I learned not from the man himself but from Stella. He often related tales of his childhood and early teen years living in Germany but was more guarded on his later life. Born at the turn of the century, Ossi was an average child growing up in prewar Germany. While serving as an apprentice the Nazis rose to power. His parents had the foresight to see the looming dangers advising their three children to leave home and make their way to a safer foreign land. They decided on Palestine, why not? It was as good a place as anywhere. The plan was for his parents to follow at a later date once their business had been sorted. They never escaped Hitler's grasp. Ossi soon became separated from his brother and sister. He struggled through the German countryside in a desperate effort for safety. Barely into his teen years with a strict and honest background, Ossi found it immensely difficult cheating, lying and stealing merely to stay alive. But this was survival. He slept in fields and barns, ate rotten fruit and vegetables on a long journey that would take him to safety in Palestine. It was on an illegal ship to Palestine, crammed with fleeing refugees of Nazi Europe,that, purely by chance he was reunited with his sister. During the cover of night the immigrants clamoured to the shores of The Holy Land.

Ossi, like many others, soon found the war did not end at the shores of their promised land. As the British army stepped up their action of stopping Jewish refugees arriving in Palestine, Ossi joined the same British army in an attempt to hold back the German advance in Africa. The Jewish brigade served with distinction, honour and great bravery. Following the second world war as had the pioneers years before, Ossi helped cultivate the barren plains near Ashkelon in the south of the country. It was there at the settlement of Avigdor he farmed cows until ill health forced retirement. Stella and Ossi entertained visitors from all over the world. Some were important politicians and diplomats, others like myself, simple house guests made to feel as important. However long our stay we were welcomed with warmth and friendship. I personally learned more about Israeli politics, the second world war and the birth of the Israeli state from Stella and Ossi than from any history book. A great believer in peace, in respect and dignity for others, Ossi was a man one did not only respect, but a man loved. I feel privileged to have known him, honoured to have been welcomed into his life and home. I was accepted into their family like one of their own, especially by daughters Ruti and Naomi.

There was no rest on visits to Stella and Ossi. I visited the basketball court where I had played with Osnat and Tal, two girls living on the moshav when I had been there for the month in 1980. Part of the Year Course scheme had involved spending a month working on a moshav. While all of my friends worked hard in the fields of their hosts, I toured the country with Stella and Ossi in their trusted Mini car. With their farm closed due to early retirement we had the opportunity to travel as I learned Israeli history from those that had lived it.

Chapter 13 The Hope

November 1984

'I swear, and commit to maintain loyalty to the State of Israel, to her laws and authorities.

To take upon myself without conditions and without reservations the responsibilities of the IDF.To obey all the commands and instructions given by the commanders and to dedicate all my strength and even to sacrifice my life for the defence of the homeland and the freedom of Israel.'

And at the call of our Lieutenant we collectively sealed what we just individually said, together, with a loud roar 'I Swear!'

One company after another sealed their oath after us. Then we each individually stood in front of our officer and accepted a gun in our right arm and a bible in our left hand that we positioned over our gun. We stood to attention as the entire crowd, soldiers and visitors sang The Hatikvah, the national anthem.

As long as the Jewish spirit is yearning deep in the heart,

With eyes turned toward the East, looking toward Zion,

Then our hope - the two-thousand-year-old hope - will not be lost:

To be a free people in our land,

The land of Zion and Jerusalem.

The words to Israel's national anthem were written in 1886 by Naphtali Herz Imber, an English poet originally from Bohemia. The melody was written by Samuel Cohen, an immigrant from Moldavia. Cohen actually based the melody on a musical theme found in Bedrich Smetana's 'Moldau.' Now here I was some two hundred years later singing the same song on my proudest day of my miserable life so far. I had grown up with the Hatikvah. It was sang at my Jewish primary school assembly along with God Save the Queen. It was sang in synagogue after services. We sang it at FZY events and other Jewish or Israel related functions but never had I felt the emotion I felt singing it here.

Jerusalem, the western wall, all that remained of the destroyed Jewish temple. The holiest city in the Jewish faith. Even a non believer like myself could not fail to be moved. Until its recapture during The Six Day War it had been administered by the Jordanian army. Jewish access to the religions holiest site was extremely limited. But what touched me more was the fact that I was now a defender of my people. The Nazis, the pogroms in Eastern Europe, the Spanish Inquisition, the Crusaders, all these butchers murdered millions of Jews who could not defend themselves. It made no difference if you were ultra religious or an atheist like myself. I hated much of the religion and so many of its principles but the simple fact was I was Jewish, like it or not. Here we were, in our own country finally with the means to defend ourselves. I thought not of synagogues and the biblical prayers but of Anne Frank, of the death camps of the Holocaust, of the Warsaw ghetto. I cried for them, the State of Israel came too late for them. But it was here now, ready for the next lot of Jews who would find themselves at the wrath of some anti-Semitic dictator. It was the Israeli army that rescued the hostages in Entebbe, Uganda, my army.

I stood proud and looked to the wall, lit up and golden. The flag of Israel flew proud in the corner. It had flown here since 1967 when my army captured Eastern Jerusalem from the Jordanians during the Six Day War. In 1897, the First Zionist Congress was held in Basel, Switzerland to consider re-establishing a homeland for Jews in Palestine. Morris Harris, a member of New York Hovevei Zion, used his awning shop to design a suitable banner and decorations for the reception, and his mother Lena Harris sewed the flag. The flag was made with two blue stripes and a large blue Star of David in the centre, the colours blue and white chosen from the design of the tallit, prayer shawl. It was accepted as the official Zionist flag at the Second Zionist Congress held in Switzerland in 1898, and the State of Israel later adopted the design as the official flag, upon declaration of Israel as an independent state in 1948. It was my flag now.

Back on Base 80 it was cleaning equipment and generally running around the toilets again. We did have our first practice on the rifle range. We found it kind of strange that we had the possession of guns for months before they taught us to shoot them. Did they not trust us? What were we going to do if confronted with terrorists? Throw philosophical arguments at them? That said, the Israelis had quite a novel method of teaching their children to swim. Throw them in a swimming pool and let instinct take over. Perhaps that was their approach to warfare. We could strip and rebuild a rifle blindfolded in seconds, we just didn't know how to fire the bastard thing.

## Chapter 14   Invisible Sun
November 22nd 1984

In the haze filled distance
I can hear the mothers cry
With only tears for resistance
She releases her child's hand
In the next street
I can hear the thud of soldiers boots
And the scampering of tiny feet
Empty shops with nothing left to loot

Clear blue skies, yet thick red rain
The air filled with violent thunder
Struck down by the hand of Cain
Hunter turned hunted turned hunter
I spy into your cell window
I can hear the cry of a dozen souls
contaminated with hatred and fear
None of us should be here

Can't we see the reflections
Of the pains of our fellow man
After horrors upon us so afflicted

shouldn't we best understand?

We were resting in our tents when the alert came in. We weren't certain if this was for real or just another exercise. Yuval, the second lieutenant and Boaz, the lieutenant, appeared with their guns and packs. Within a few minutes we were on a bus, fully equipped and on maneuver. Nerves were on edge. We were excited, and frightened as the bus headed to the West Bank town of Tulkarem. During the Six Day War of in June 1967 Tulkarm was captured by the Israeli army, The city of around 40,000, almost exclusively Moslem Palestinian Arabs, is situated on the western edge of northern West Bank, about 15 kilometres west of Nablus and 15 kilometres east of the Israeli coastal city of Netanya. The Arabic name, which translates as 'the long place of the vineyard' is derived from the Aramaic words Toor Karma, meaning "mount of vineyards. Today the population is almost entirely Muslim. Prior to Israel's occupation of the city in 1967, there were an estimated 1,000 Christians living in Tulkarm, but roughly half of the community emigrated in the aftermath of the war, while most of the remaining Christians gradually emigrated afterward. Accounts differ on the reason for the decline of the Christian population. Some say they were forced out by the Jews, others say the majority Moslem population forced them out. A third theory is that they simply moved to areas in the new state with a larger Christian demographic population.

There are around 160,000 Christians living in Israel, about 2% of the population living as citizens with freedom of religion, rule of law and open elections. Christians can move anywhere, even building a number of churches recently in Tel Aviv. The government safeguards the Christian holy places and is lenient on the right of return of Christian refugees. The Christian churches own a significant part of Jerusalem, including the land on which the Knesset sits. Their greatest problem often comes from the Muslims. A growing minority, especially in the north, are virulently anti-Christian, using physical attacks, provocative speech and seditious billboards. While Bethlehem was once 90% Christian, today it is 65% Muslim. 60% more Christians live in Israel than in the Palestinian territories. A small new Christian party, B'nai Brith, calls on its youth to serve in the Israeli army and hundreds each year do so. Its leader, Reverend Nadaff, declares, "We love this country."

Israeli Christians have several problems. One is lacking the benefits given to Israelis who serve in the army. Another is the provocative defacing and vandalising of Christian monuments and cemeteries by groups of radical Jews. Israel is the only place in the Middle East where the Christians are growing in number. They are excelling in education, doing well in business and feeling relatively safe from their radical tormentors.

We would see the whites of the eyes of the enemy. There was unrest and rioting in the town and our role was to help enforce a curfew and restore order. The few days in Tulkarem offered a good insight into the real army. The whole town had been placed under a 24 hour curfew. There was just one road in and out of the town and we manned the checkpoints. We guarded in rolling four hour shifts, few attempted to cross the barrier, fewer were successful. Yossi, our sergeant was tough and uncompromising. He seemed cold and unsympathetic to the pleads of the locals to cross the checkpoint. That was until a taxi pulled up in the dead of the night. laden with a heavily pregnant woman, crying in pain.

'Fuck the rules' he barked waving the car through.

The town was poor and looked it. Our base was the local police station, a remnant from British Mandate times of the 1940s. We patrolled in groups of half a dozen searching suspicious looking locals. Problem was most looked suspicious. As we rested on some open ground an old lady approached us with a tray of food. In hindsight we should have refused, who knows what she may have given us, but we were hungry and the lamb and pita bread looked a lot more appetising than the canned meat back at base. If I have one abiding memory of Tulkarem, and all Arab villages I 'visited' during my service, it is of the dead quiet nights save the constant barking of dogs. For years afterwards, whenever I heard a dog barking at night I thought back to Tulkarem. Our patrols of the centre of the town were intended to be 'provocative' and 'to show the bastards who was boss' according to Yuval, our officer. Any doubts that Yuval was an immature, complete arsehole would later be confirmed. Onlookers spied us from their windows with intimidating hatred. The streets were pretty much deserted. The shops had pulled down their shutters the previous day and they now remained shut. A general strike closed all the businesses and the local services including the schools. Sporadically groups of small children would appear from some side street and begin to verbally abuse us. At least I presume they were insults, as my command of Arabic was non existent. In a couple of areas tyres were set alight and the air filled with thick black smoke. The officers feared a full scale riot. That would bring the Israeli, but more damaging the International press. It would also bring more senior officers and a real bollocking for Yuval.

I don't know what had caused the curfew. It was usually following a violent event like a murder or terrorist attack inside Israel. Collective punishment was the policy of the

Israeli government. A terrorists home was evacuated and demolished no matter who else lived there. Their home town was put in lockdown for a time also preventing residents from going out to work. Political debates were not allowed in the army. Soldiers and officers kept their beliefs to themselves. As the saying goes, ours was not to question why but to do or die. Looking back it was a dangerous mission in Tulkarem. We were barely soldiers, just a few months served and had completed very limited training. Our duty in Petach Tikvah park could hardly be classed as active duty. All it took was for us to be confronted by an angry mob of schoolchildren, one soldier opens fire and suddenly an international incident.

There were no clear lines here. Yes the army had rules for engagement. You only shoot when your life or your fellow soldiers are in danger. You aim for the lower part of the body at first and only shoot to kill if the danger continues. Those were the rules in the classroom, it was very different and real on the street. And what about following orders? When did you refuse, if at all? Were we simply an army who followed every order without question? Did we question but still follow the orders? Can a nation survive if every soldier just decided for himself what action to take? So why bother with officers. What if you fired and killed a child or baby? What if you didn't fire and the terrorist detonated a bomb killing your comrades? How could you live with either scenario and how did you decide in a fraction of a second? Experience, something we certainly didn't have, may have helped a little, but in reality we were fucked. There were incidents where officers ordered their soldiers to open fire in contravention of Israeli military rules and guidelines. The soldiers complied with the orders. Later the officers were stripped of their command and the soldiers jailed. Justice served in a humane army but the damage already done with a dead civilian. Palestinian terrorism started with the terrorist leaving a bomb on a bus or in a waste bin on a busy street and later escalated to pregnant women, carrying a child with a bomb strapped to her waist. She would walk into a crowd of Israelis and detonate the explosive killing herself, innocent civilians and her child or baby. If placing bombs and running were wrong, how immoral and evil to take your innocent child with you to meet Allah. The terrorists would say that this is all that is left to them to win their fight for freedom. I say there can be nothing more sick and evil. The Palestinian terrorists say they will stop when the Israelis retreat, the Israelis say they will retreat when the terrorists stop. Stalemate.

Three months before I had felt the immense pride of donning my uniform but right now I wanted to return to my shorts and U2 T shirt. I felt uncomfortable at what I was doing. Were we naive in blindly following orders? Were we naive in believing the locals wanted peace? None of us were sure what side we should be on. What most of us did know was these few days didn't feel right.


Chapter 15 Mother

December 1st 1984

Most of the garin had friends around the country and visited them on free weekends. We would mostly try and coordinate our visits back to Kfar Blum so to be together at specific weekends. This particular weekend we had decided to all meet up but changed our minds at the last minute. I decided to visit Kibbutz Tzuba near Jerusalem where I had started my Israel journey. I met up with Shmulik and Dikla and a brief reunion with Gila. Reuven looked especially impressed with his protegee. I felt good again. Reuven had offered me a guest room on the kibbutz but I politely declined the offer instead sharing with Gila. It was good to reacquaint, if only for a couple of nights.

On the Saturday afternoon I took the short walk to old Crusader ruins at the edge of the kibbutz. I sat and looked at the Jerusalem hills as I had done nine months earlier. Nothing had changed, but then I felt quite stupid, nothing had changed in two thousand years, what could change in nine months? I watched an eagle cruise above a neighbouring hill. I listened to the winter wind crash against the biblical mountains. I hoped it would snow, I had never seen Jerusalem in the snow. I noticed Gila coming towards me then stop. She must have realised I needed this time alone. She half waved before turning around and walking back to her house. I felt alone but I wasn't sure if I was happy with that feeling. I couldn't decide.

News from England came via mail or a monthly phone call paid for by the army. Not only were our letters through the army read and monitored, our phone calls were also monitored through the army operator. As if we were party to any top secret information. I would play down any real details when phoning my family. I didn't want to worry them. Most of the time we were training and out of harms way and risk free. The few times we were in danger there was no point in adding any undue worry to our loved ones so far away. I would call my family most weekends I got out. The arrangement was that I would call them collect, they would reject the request to accept the charges and call me straight back. My mother though, bless her, became so excited on answering the call, always accepted the charges. In the end I gave up explaining the plan.

International Operator 'Hello, this is Israel, I have a call from Johnny Wallman, do you accept the charges?'

My mother 'Yes, Yes, Hi Johnny'

Myself 'Mum, I told you, refuse the call and call me back, I'm here by the phone, I'd answer straight away'

'It's fine, Gary, Gary, it's Johnny on the phone' she would shout down the phone half deafening me.

My father, asleep in the television room with the TV blaring, picks up the other phone. Now I have both of them throwing questions.

'Are you OK? We saw there was a bomb in Jerusalem' my mother asks.

'Nita, he's fine, he's not in Jerusalem and he's talking to us, he must be OK' replies my father.

'But it's only a small country, he's near Jerusalem' worries my mother

'Nita, he's on a kibbutz nowhere near fucking Jerusalem' my father shouts.

The man had no patience and struggled sometimes with my mothers naivety. 'Anita' became 'Nita' when he got angry.

The call lasted a good ten minutes before I got involved. While they knew a fair amount about Israel much of their knowledge came only from the television news. I would feel uneasy. My father wanted to ask me real questions about how things really were but was afraid to do so. Any negative comments would only worry my mother. He left the talking to my mother.

'What time is it there?' she asks. My father loses it again.

'Why do you need to know, are you going out there?' he shouts

They start arguing again and I divert the conversation.

'We all got watermelons and avocado's on the kibbutz today' I said

'I didn't know you liked avocado's' replied my mother.

'Does it really matter Nita?' shouts my father.

'How is everybody there, Suzy, Paul?' I ask taking yet another diversion.

My mother is now on track. I get a rundown of everybody from my siblings to the staff in the shops to the gardener. She is in her element.

'Is there anything you need sending?' asks my father returning to more practical matters.

'I like the packages you send with the newspaper and chocolate, that's all, I'm fine' I reply.

The conversation lasts at least fifteen minutes and runs a little thin.

'OK, best go now, there's a queue for the phone' I lie.

'OK son, be safe' says my dad

'Bye love' says my mum who is now crying.

I'm not sure the phone call helped anyone really.

Meanwhile the boys in blue had returned to their erratic form losing to Shrewsbury and Middlesborough, drawing three games and eeking out narrow victories over Birmingham and Blackburn. A big improvement in form was needed.

## Chapter 16 If I Die For You
December 9th 1984

The desert sun broke our fragile backs
The officer broke our shattered spirits
All in the name of courage and honour
We'd dug the hole, now time to fill it
We were not kids with freckles and spots
Our mature feet blistered in the sand
Heavy packs filled with bullets and regrets
Certainly didn't feel like holy land

Through the barbed wire and nettles
We crawled, cursed and cried
Drew blood into the biblical sand
Taken to the edge of our minds
We climbed the imposing sand dune
To be confronted by yet another
Our minds the only enemy in sight
We became a band of brothers

Our uniforms drenched with sweat and toil
Our boots close to melting
The officer baulked out his commands

'Grenade, pull the bastard ring!'
We attacked the enemy position
Released rapid fire
Took cover behind the desert bushes
Called for air cover on the wire

Sunday morning, December seventh
All so quiet on the base
Suddenly, news filters
One man down, one bullet, one sad waste
Stuart fell in the early hours
Not by the enemy slain
But by his own hand, his own gun
Burdened by his internal pain

Together we beat the desert sands
Together we cried the tears of pain
Together we stood against the 'army of the people'
Together we cried his name.

Our final two months of basic training took us Moshave Sade
in the southern Negev desert. Forty kilometres south of
BeerSheba. This place was well and truly the end of the world.
Our training area provided more than its fair share of hills,
nettles, snakes and scorpions. Add to that the dust and the sand.

The desert also became very cold at night. Night training was carried out in almost freezing conditions. Between exercises we would huddle together for some scant warmth. Meanwhile the days were often unbearably hot even this late in the year. Every now and again an ice cream van would turn up on base. It was the strangest thing, not exactly as if we were on his route. If the officers consented, and often they didn't, we were allowed to purchase ice cream and cold drinks. I had never liked chocolate flavoured milk, strawberry yes, I could drink that until the cows came home, but not chocolate. Today however, with the absence of anything strawberry, I tasted sweet nectar in the form of chocolate milk. As the sun beat down on my heavy shoulders I ripped open the bag of milk with my teeth, spat out the plastic corner onto the sandy ground and gulped back the nectar. Mealtimes in the desert were not quite fine dining. Everything came with added sand. Breakfast consisted of warm black coffee, semi stale bread, jam and hard boiled eggs. Lunch and dinner were usually, almost always, no in fact always chicken and rice. Even our small mess tins still looked sad and empty once the food had been dumped inside. We were always hungry. Whatever snacks we had brought from home were usually consumed by the second day back at base.

Most of us were at a low ebb by now. Our officer Yuval had issues. He appeared to over compensate for his small stature and young age, especially some of those in our platoon were over thirty years old. He appeared to suffer from classic small dick syndrome. Throughout our training there had been complaints about some of his actions. While we understood the importance of 'tough love' he failed to understand we were more savvy to much of his bullshit. Todd seemed to suffer more than most. Well built and tough looking, Todd was tasked with carrying the heavy machine gun. He struggled with knee problems but his complaints fell on deaf ears. He was often unfairly disciplined, more than often being kept back on base when the rest of the platoon were allowed home at weekends. Many of us suffered less but still had to endure Yuvals childish sarcasm and petty bullying mainly over our poor knowledge of the language. He often used street slang to baffle us with the language trying to show us up in front of the other soldiers. In reality his lack of professionalism put the whole platoon in danger.

Our orders were always to be back on base by 10am Sunday morning following our weekends away. It was almost eleven when we noticed Malcolm only just returning. Malcolm stopped at the entrance of the base to talk to Yuval for a few minutes before walking to us. It was around a six hour journey from Kfar Blum to the base and we assumed that Malcolm had simply missed the connection arriving late. He summoned the Garin members together inside the tent. It seemed ominous as he began crying.

'I'm sorry guys, I'm sorry, Stuart killed himself on the kibbutz last night'. Dumbstruck we filtered from the tent. We were all now in tears. The other soldiers in the platoon, not in our garin, came over to console us as they heard the news. Todd punched a nearby iron bar. We were a mess and in no way competent to function, least of all as soldiers. Reuven from a different garin took control as our spokesman with his fluent Hebrew. We requested an urgent meeting with Yuval. He clearly knew the nature of the requested meeting as Malcolm had already talked to him when returning to the base. He kept us waiting over an hour for the meeting. He knew we were there, in the army, in the middle of the desert, in pain with no family. The garin was our family and we had lost one of our family members and Yuval was more interested in pushing his authority.

A crowd, which perhaps could have been viewed upon as a mob, gathered outside the officers tent. Yuval re-emerged from his tent but with Reuven continuing his role as spokesman we demanded to speak to Boaz, Yuvals senior. What little respect the entire platoon had for Yuval had now dangerously dissipated. His immaturity and poor judgment shone as he refused the few of us from the garin permission to return to the kibbutz for a few days where all our group could be together. Boaz refused to meet with us, an action he would later apologise for. Meanwhile what transpired was similar to a cattle market as both sides bartered how many people could leave and for how long. We were given 24 hour leave to make the fourteen hour round trip. Once the first two had returned the second two could leave. Myself and Todd cried almost the entire journey back. We must have been some sight sat in the front seats across from the driver but we didn't care. I wasn't sure what hurt more, the loss of Stuart or the uncaring, callous attitude of Yuval and the so called peoples army. The girls met us as we got off the bus and our tears flowed again. We only had a few hours together, it was already late in the night and early the next morning we would be back on the bus back to base. One thing the army did teach us was it was worth taking a fourteen hour round trip to spend three or four hours with the ones you love.


Chapter 17 Mad World

December 15th 1984

One thing Yuval had not bargained on, or did not understand, was how tight a group the garin to Kfar Blum felt. We were family and while much of the time we argued and bickered, during a crisis we rallied together. Murmurings around the platoon were now becoming open dissent and belligerent contempt. Yuval decided to exert more power. He cancelled planned leave for the entire platoon resulting in the garin missing a planned memorial service on the kibbutz for Stuart. Many of the other soldiers in the platoon, not in our garin, had also wanted to attend the memorial, others were just pissed off that had lost their weekend off. News reached the girls on kibbutz that we would not be back for the weekend memorial. Within a few hours a large black 4x4 vehicle, horn blaring, sped into the base. Sand blew through the hot air as it came to a screeching halt in the centre of the base. Yuvals attempt to discharge the vehicle was met with a torrent of abuse from the girls of Garin Nesher. If they couldn't have the guys at the memorial on Kfar Blum, they would have the memorial here in the middle of the Negev desert. Yuval finally retreated. One of the benefits of Nahal and the garin structure was the fortnightly 'Yom Garinim', Garin Day, where members of the garin not serving with us would make a two hour visit. With them arrived mail from home, food packages from our adopted families and most importantly huge moral support. We would picnic and chat, exchange important information and gossip. This visit was not scheduled, not authorised and for fear of his safety, not broken up by Yuval.

The army response to our loss was to invite the army shrink to work the voodoo that they do. Nobody cooperated. One by one we sat through our individual session in silence. It was not some mumbo jumbo physco analysis we needed, just a few hours together to grieve. The girls stayed a couple of hours. The officers and army doctor retreated. It all became a little bit surreal. The garin members would all be sat in one tent, talking, laughing, crying as one by one we would be called into a different tent for our session with the army head shrink.

'How do you feel?' he asked ..... no response

'Explain your feelings' he continued .... no response. After half a dozen questions and a brief lecture on the pain of losing someone close and after no response to any of the questions I think he realised he was beaten. I think Todd was the only one to respond by telling him to fuck off. We were confused. This was not the caring army, the Israel Defence Force we thought we had joined. It appeared that we were not only defending the nation, our fight was not only with occupied Arabs but also with our own officers.

Yuval began his retaliation for the blatant undermining of his fragile command. Todd was denied leave indefinitely. While this was clearly against army rules by the time his complaint was heard he had been confined to base for well over a month. I was to be kept back on base as the majority of the platoon were to take up a brief role in Lebanon. Our objections fell on deaf ears. I swallowed my pride and half pleaded with Yuval to let me go. He told me I wasn't ready as a soldier yet, smiled and walked off. We all knew I was as ready as most of the others. I hated that bastard. With a bruised ego I settled down to a week on base, one small consolation being the absence of Yuval. His reasoning, not being ready and my poor Hebrew, failed to stack up as others with a worse knowledge did travel. He often selected various individuals for personal bullying including Todd. Malcolm, Moshe and others. It was becoming more and more likely that in the event of any future fire-fight with the enemy he would be the first to be shot, by any one of his thirty soldiers.

As it happened we had a fantastic week on the base. Around ten soldiers remained on base with one sergeant who spent the bulk of the week at a nearby kibbutz with his girlfriend. We took it in turns to take in a day trip shopping at the Bedouin market in BeerSheba and patrolling the base on a wild donkey we managed to catch and tame. One of these days I used my 'Lone Soldier' status to request a day to sort out my banking in Tel Aviv. I did genuinely have issues to sort but in truth they would have waited until my next leave. I spent my day off in Tel Aviv, an hour at the bank and the rest of the morning wandering around town. I enjoyed lunch at a chic cafe on Rehov Dizengoff. I watched the world go by as I tucked into my steak and chips washed down with a cool Goldstar beer. Tel Aviv was so alive and vibrant. It had everything from the cosmopolitan chic of Dizengoff to the seedy back streets next to the bus station. There you could purchase any manor of fake items, copy tapes, fake Levi jeans and tracksuits with the name 'NOKE' emblazoned on the front. I watched the Israeli girls strut past as I tucked into my steak. Every one a bronzed goddess with a huge ego and an attitude. I think I fell in love a hundred times.

By early afternoon I was a little bored but it was too early to return to base. On the corner of Ben Yehuda Street was a porn cinema. Advertising half price for soldiers, the offer was too good to refuse. I paid and took a seat mid way back in the cinema. It was dark and was a rolling movie. Once it ended the lights would come on and after a ten minute break, the movie would play again. This was maybe to give the viewers a chance to purchase tissues. I got in just a few minutes before the end of the movie somewhat unhappy because I now knew how it ended. I was upset that the housewife never seemed to marry the plumber in the end. And why did she always leave her shoes on? And why high heels in the house, surely that was uncomfortable when doing the housework. The lights came on and I turned around to see what type of person would come to this kind of place, besides perverts like myself. Behind me, half a dozen rows back sat a red faced Peter. I laughed as he nervously shuffled to the exit. He never told anyone of our encounter, but I did. I'm not sure he ever forgave me for that indiscretion.

It had been a week since the white, army Renault car had pulled up at our near deserted base. The officer read out a list of soldiers to be taken to a medics course in Tel Aviv. Problem was everybody on the list were in Lebanon. The officer, unfazed by this minor hiccup demanded that four soldiers join him anyway. Our objections fell upon deaf ears. Within half an hour four of us were on our way to the army medics course at Base Tsrifin near Tel Aviv. It was insane. It didn't matter who attended an army course as long as the particular branch did not lose its representation. Our poor Hebrew, one soldiers broken army and my fear of needles seemed to be no barrier to joining the course. Three times I met with the course officer. At first I explained that I didn't think my Hebrew would be good enough to get me through the course.

'Don't worry, we will help you through' he replied. Our protests fell on deaf ears for almost a week until finally one by one we were allowed to quit the course, my time came on the day we were due to practice injections. The doctors training us had been supportive and friendly. They had offered support to our problems but now the penny dropped and a medic with a fear of needles was not really the ideal medic during battle. Finally the officer in charge relented and I was released back to my unit. If this entire episode had not been bizarre enough, then sitting on the lawn of the base listening to the annual queens speech on the BBC just about closed yet another strange episode in the army. As her majesty thanked the Commonwealth for their loyal support the base administrator handed me a blank, signed pass and I was free to leave. With no dates written on the pass I decided to return to the kibbutz for a couple of days before returning to the company at Moshave Sade.

It was during my time at Moshave Sade that I became quite ill. It was during one of the many equipment inspections that I felt weak and faint. Following a check up from the medic I was sent to the army hospital in Tel Aviv. A week of blood tests brought no diagnoses. Although it was nice to eat food that didn't contain sand, I was getting bored and missing my comrades. Feeling better, I checked myself out of the hospital and late in the afternoon decided to return to the base at Moshave Sade.It was almost dark as the bus arrived at Beer Sheba from Tel Aviv. I had not thought this out properly. How would I get from the bus station to the base? And in the dark. I began walking from the junction into the desert. My outstretched hitchhiking arm somewhat redundant as nothing passed my way. I was getting desperate now as the hour passed into two. This was Arab country. Beduin Arabs were mostly friendly to Israelis, many served in the Israeli army but still this really wasn't the place for a soldier to be wandering about alone. With several bases in the area I couldn't believe no army vehicles had passed this way. I was becoming anxious as a white pick up truck appeared from the distance and pulled up beside me. An elderly Beduin man dressed in traditional clothes and a red kafia leaned over opening the passenger door.

'Do you know the army base at Moshave Sade?' I asked nervously in English accented Hebrew.

'You shouldn't really be walking out here alone' he replied in Arab accented Hebrew.

'Why is it dangerous' I asked

'A little but not so much that, it's a long walk to your base' he said smiling.

I jumped in the open door. He knew roughly where the bases were and offered to drop me off. It was a good thirty minute journey along a dark road through the mountains. I was terrified but relieved to be getting back. He seemed amused by my naivety. We passed a couple of bases before I spotted a sign with the Nahal emblem.

'It must be here' I announced. 'shukran, thank you,' I said as I climbed down from the truck.

As he drove off into the night and I walked towards my comrades I imagined the Beduin man returning to his camp and sat around a camp fire laughing with his fellow tribesmen.

'Hey I just had this dumb fuck Israeli soldier in my truck. He was wandering the desert in the middle of the night. Dumb Jews, forty years wandering the desert wasn't enough for them, they want more.'


Chapter 18 When Johnny Comes Marching Home

January 19th 1985


I have felt the fear, I have felt the faith

I have felt the pain, Seen the look of terror upon your face

I have felt life, I have felt death

I have felt love, Seen you touch with pride your hollow chest

I have seen the cheats, I have seen the honour

I have felt the anger, Seen the hatred consume our waking hours

I have felt the peace, I have seen closed doors

I have walked open fields, I have marched with the flag of war

I have felt the hope, I have felt the despair

I have seen your tears fall, As I ran my fingers through your tangled hair

I have turned away, I have closed my eyes

Yet the tears still escape, My ears still burn with all of your lies.

The new year began with a certain amount of guarded enthusiasm. Basic training was drawing to a close and while our next six months of Batash, more extensive training, would be tough, at least it would be without the child that was Yuval. Or at least that was what we thought. At least for now we would have a weeks holiday. Beforehand the Masa Kumta, beret march, was the final hike in a long series of hikes undertaken throughout basic training. The Masa Kumta was when you earned your brigade's beret, which was simply a different colour from other brigades. Our beret was black in colour. The marches build up in distance from a couple of kilometres in the first few days to a full forty kilometres at the end. The main purpose of the hike was obvious, you do them in combat. Not every battle is fought right outside your front door. Sometimes you have to hike a few miles out there, and a few back. The use of stretchers loaded up were also to simulate battle conditions. The hikes also built teamwork. Two single file lines in strict formation and mostly at night. Complete silence. Full combat gear including combat vest with all related equipment, machine gun, heavy machine gun, water packs and stretchers, sometimes opened carrying soldiers. Conducted at a fast pace anywhere from flat fields, to the beach shore line to steep mountains.

The hike was awful and it hurt. Few of us shared the enthusiasm of the officers, especially Yuval. This was the big event of our basic training. It was cup final day. Many of the soldiers were excited and raring to go. I was terrified but I was hopeful to get through it from the first step. I didn't want to do it but knew I had to at least try. It was a challenge, a milestone in our army lives. Every soldier carried something extra other than their own equipment be it the radio, heavy machine gun, ammunition for that gun, stretchers or water pack. There were several dilemmas on what to carry. The stretcher and radio were a constant heavy weight while the water pack was a lot heavier at the start but got lighter as the hike went on as soldiers used the water to refill their own water bottles. The heavy machine gun was just too heavy at any time. All this was largely academic as the officers allocated the equipment. I was given the water pack. The pack weighed around forty pounds, held around sixteen litres of water and leaked. It leaked enough to give me an uncomfortable wet patch on my back but not enough to lighten the load. The previous hikes were all conducted in silence. With officers at the front and back the silence was mostly observed though we did talk quietly sometimes. The Beret Hike was a noisy affair. We were encouraged to talk, laugh (fat chance in that much pain) and even sing. The song telling the story of four and twenty virgins that had travelled down from Inverness was quite popular.

The first ten kilometres were tough, then it just got even harder. I felt every small stone through my boot. My toes felt like they were glued together, my right knee felt as if it had jumped out of its socket and joined its friend in the left knee. By the 10 kilometre mark around half a dozen had quit. My socks were wet with sweat, my back wet from the water pack. I prayed for each hourly water stop. I begged soldiers to fill their bottles from my pack rather than others. I promised them the world. I don't know if the pain was real or in my mind. There was no fatigue, I wasn't tired. I was just in immense pain. A couple of us spent five kilometres recalling luxury food from home. We listed every chocolate bar invented, cooked and devoured every meal in our minds. Imaginary steak and chips, fish, chips and mushy peas, cheese and onion crisps, Cadbury dairy milk chocolate. We did all we could to take our minds off the hike. The talcum powder sprinkled liberally in my socks and underwear was of no help whatsoever. My feet were sweating litres, my balls were drenched. It was the early hours of the morning, almost dawn, when we hit the twenty five kilometre point. My knee finally went as we climbed yet another hill, quickly followed by what little willpower I had remaining. This wasn't worth it anymore, not for a fucking beret anyway, and one I could buy in the army store the following day. I felt the rocks underfoot pierce through my boots. My knee pounded. There were times during every hike when you argued with yourself. Was the pain real or my imagination. You hit the wall. Was the wall really that high or were you just imagining it so high? Often in past hikes there had been an officer or another soldier close by that would grab your shirt or belt and drag you forward a few yards in order to give you a fresh momentum. I had no one on that occasion. There were other soldiers around me but they too were struggling. They needed the drag through as much as I did. This was no longer a march. The hundred or soldiers were scattered everywhere. The front runners were a good few kilometres ahead, there were stragglers a few kilometres behind. Soldiers were running, others almost crawling. Rest and pee breaks were not organised any longer. Had this been a battle march then by the time those at the rear would have made it to the point of conflict, the few at the front would probably have been killed and the battle long over. This time I knew the pain was real. I hobbled to the nearest officer explaining my knee had buckled and I wanted to quit. Surprisingly he offered no objection, nor did he try any encouragement. He pointed me in the direction of the army truck following us and I climbed inside joining the few dozen or so other soldiers who had also given up the ghost. I felt no shame in not having completed the hike, perhaps that was my problem in the first half of the army. I think I had done my best. I did feel a little out of it at the celebrations at the end but I convinced myself that for my poor fitness, my twenty five kilometres was equal to others forty. And in the end we all received the black beret, whatever distance we covered.

Manchester City were on a roll. Six victories and two draws from nine games saw City back amongst the leaders at the top. Coventry had put us out of the FA Cup in the third round, Chelsea had hammered us out of the League Cup earlier. Now we could concentrate on the league, on promotion. City manager, McNeil, had brought in some quality players at affordable prices not least Derek Parlane on a free transfer who netted nineteen goals for the season.

Back on base and the office politics began with a huge ironic twist. Each garin was required to put forward a certain percentage of its soldiers towards officers course. The list was submitted to the army and almost always approved. Of course nothing was simple with Garin Nesher and our list was ripped up by Yuval. He completed his own list when he discovered he would be staying with the platoon. He decided to off-load some of his least favourite including Ian and Moshe. Others, highly suitable for officers course, and willing to move on, were turned down. Again our protests fell upon deaf ears. Boaz again appeared to support his junior officer but Yuval was sailing close to the wind.

The 'Passing Out' parade signalled the end of basic training and followed a full week of preparation and drill rehearsing. Our dress uniforms were even dry cleaned and neatly pressed. Perhaps as a symbol of our less than heroic en devours of basic training, the heavens opened with incessant showers. Like drowned rats we were forced to change into our reserve uniforms. That said, no thunder-storms would stop us celebrating our graduation. Busses arrived on base by the dozen. Each was filled with laughing, proud parents and families. All but one headed for the parade ground and the seating erected for the occasion. The lone parent was my father, not one to embrace conformity. How he found our platoon in the middle of the entire base is still a mystery to this day. I watched in both joy and horror as he approached the sergeant drilling us. The balking sergeant turned to talk to this infiltrator, smiled, and called me out. My father hugged me in front of my fellow troops. I felt no embarrassment, just immense pride. In front of the parading soldiers our families and friends cheered, applauded and endured the thunderous rain. My father had attended with Stella. I had no idea either would be present beforehand. I could not see them now in the crowd but I felt them watching. I felt their pride. After my academic failure, after years of wandering without ambition, finally I had made my family proud. As we launched our black berets into the wet, Tel Aviv sky, I smiled as never before.


Our Army Family

To explain the entire structure of the army would be a novel in itself and probably only serve as an effective cure to insomniacs. We served in the Nahal unit. Nahal was favoured by many new immigrants who had no family in Israel. The kibbutz offered a home for the soldiers on weekends leave from the army. Our training was as rigorous as other infantry branches of the army. Although our service was a few months shorter than in other units that time difference was spent on kibbutz, technically we were still soldiers during that time and sometimes called away for training exercises. The Nahal unit was made up of many garinim (groups) each affiliated to a particular kibbutz. For some unknown reason our garin was affiliated to two different kibbutzim. Kfar Blum in the north and Ketura in the Arava desert. Coincidentally I had stayed on Ketura for six months during my year in Israel a few years previously. There was no love lost between the two groups with only Erika from Ketura forming any friendship with the Kfar Blum members. When the Ketura members threw a party to celebrate the end of basic training the entire platoon except those from Kfar Blum were invited. Unfortunately for the Ketura group, we found out via Erika and crashed the party. We were the 'bit of rough'.

Other garinim included Zalaf featuring Danny, probably the only man who played the army game and won, and Alberto who arrived from South America in his teens and avoided the army call up for years. Unfortunately for him, the time calculated for your length of service is calculated from the time you enter the country, not the time you join up. At age thirty six Alberto was forced to serve the full three years national service.We joked that on completing his service he would be issued with his pension card rather than his discharge papers. At least he would be too old to do Miluim we told him. It seemed that the members of Garin Zalaf had the same warped sense of humour as our garin. Our garin name derived from a diving, copulating eagle. 'Zalaf' spelt out 'Ze Lo Picnic', 'this is no picnic'. How true. Then there were the religious guys. Ultra religious citizens can avoid serving in the army, much to the wrath of most secular Israelis. These guys, to their credit, followed the conscience and served with us. If we were a group of complete misfits, they were not far behind. There were the sensible ones, Jeremy, Mike (another Mancunian) and Lawrence. Gideon and Eddie bickered like a married couple. Myself, Ian and Jeff often combined to make a comedy trio. It kept us, and everyone else sane. Andy and Dave, originally from London, now from a kibbutz in the Galilee, also behaved like a married couple although less dysfunctional than Gideon and Eddie. Ian had applied to join our garin at Kfar Blum but had been rejected much to my annoyance.

The girls of Kfar Blum were close to civil war from the start. Jo and Susan constantly and unfairly appeared to bear the wrath of Janet and Yaffa while sweet Yael perched on the fence unwilling and unable to upset anybody. Meanwhile Laura did upset almost everyone. She appeared to take everything much more seriously than everybody else. Of course all this was serious stuff but sometimes we needed to be stupid and reckless. This wasn't her way. The menfolk were somewhat more refined, well a little anyway. Numbers were reducing at an alarming rate. Kenny had left the platoon and kibbutz, as had Stuart obviously. Peter had left the platoon but remained on the kibbutz. We were now five in the platoon, myself, Todd, Malcolm, Moshe and Jeff. That number was soon to be reduced quite dramatically.

Chapter 19 Nowhere to Run to

February 3rd 1985

Anybody who had served in the army knew Takoa, and the directions. Go to the end of the world and turn right. Takoa, around ten kilometres west of Jerusalem made Moshave Sade look like Butlins Holiday Camp. The base stood in a valley between an Arab village and Jewish settlement. While Moshave Sade provided sand and dust, Takoa provided rocks and dust. In fairness there were also a fair amount of trees and vegetation. Following a weekend home, the unit would meet up in Jerusalem at the Binyenei Ha'Uma international conference centre . Buses lined the road waiting to transport soldiers to their relevant bases. Across the street stood a food van that served the best omelet in a bread roll. A little treat before our return to hell. Our training consisted of practicing an attack on enemy positions. Mission suicide we called it. The idea that three men would attack a heavily armed gun post shouting 'Esh Esh' or 'Fire Fire' seemed ridiculous but hey Yuval knows best. Myself and Ian, now thoroughly pissed off with everything army took a turn at being the defenders of the post. Mockingly we made ricochet noises instead of the usual

'Esh Esh'. Our officers were not impressed especially as our comrades fell about laughing during their assault.

Perhaps our biggest horror was the reappearance of Yuval. In theory he should have been promoted and moved on to another unit but instead he remained a second lieutenant and retained his poor command. Immediately Todd requested foreign leave. Soldiers with family abroad can return to their home country for three weeks, almost all would stretch that visit to four weeks. Yuval was powerless to stop him. This was going to be a long long six months. Early in Batash we were involved in the Battalion manouvres. The exercise had been the culmination of endless planning. It appeared to us that its success, or failure, could impact hugely on the future careers of our officers. Yuval's stress levels reached record heights. We were told that all kinds of top politicians and generals would be observing our ability to wage war. Tanks and helicopters would be involved. This was our own NATO exercise. As it turned out, we simply ran from one bunker to a second, and then a third shooting live ammunition. After days of cleaning our equipment, which became dirty within minutes of jumping inside a muddy bunker and hours of lectures on the importance of the exercise, it was all over with a damp squib. It was like the girl you had wanted for years, for you to be finally lying next to her and for you to empty your rifle before you even got your pants down. It was a huge anti climax. Of the exercise, we never saw the bigger picture. We heard the tanks but we were a small part of the big thing. We were, perhaps unfairly, suitably unimpressed by the whole thing. We hadn't really done a great deal. Maybe if we had watched a film of the event afterwards we would have had a different opinion. However, that said, the officers were happy, it had been a huge success. It was certain that Arab nations surrounding our tiny state were simply quivering in their army boots watching this Nahal exercise. Any invasion plans now put firmly on hold made the country a little safer for the moment.

Training generally seemed a little inadequate. Israel has fought wars in 1948, 1956, 1967 and 1973. it has performed incursions into Lebanon, Gaza and The West Bank. The country cannot afford to lose a war and never has done. Obviously they are doing something right. I just didn't see what it was. This was nothing like the movies but then perhaps real war was nothing like the movies. We never dug a trench, we never hacked through jungle with huge machetes. Instead, in groups of three and then six and then thirty six, we attacked a circular mound occupied by imaginary soldiers. We ran across open fields towards this enemy position. Probably in real war we would have had air cover, but even so, it seemed like assisted suicide.

With Todd in America, Ian and Moshe at officers course and Jeff on special duties training (commandos) only myself and Malcolm remained in the platoon from our garin. We were both excluded from further training and forced to spend all training time on guard duty. Yuval was later reprimanded for this action. We felt like two housewives at home waiting for our male folk to return home from work. Yuval continued his relentless bullying and belittlement of his soldiers. Eventually his day came when he became the ridicule of the unit.

On his first night exercise Yuval managed to get the platoon lost in the mountains most of the night. Frantically he called for help, myself and Malcolm laughing hysterically on the radio as Boaz attempted to guide him back to base. The air was filled with expletives as the loud radio broadcast Boaz screaming at Yuval. I doubt I could have completed the task but then I wasn't an officer. There was a serious aspect to this failure. There is a story, I don't know how accurate, but even if it is untrue it is still possible, of an officer during a conflict. The young and inexperienced officer, leading several men on a dark, moonless night, gets lost but is embarrassed to admit it. Without realising it he leads part of his platoon in a circle. When he spots silhouettes in the distance he orders his troops to fire believing they are the enemy. They were his own soldiers. Six young boys, soldiers, were killed. The irony was that a few months earlier these and other soldiers had written to the battalion commander stating that the officer often got them lost on hikes and was unsafe. The letter was ignored. The soldiers should never had died. Thank god we never heard this story while Yuval was with us. Thank god we never had to go into battle with him.

Boaz was a decent guy. One rank higher than Yuval, probably a year or two older but a whole lot more mature. While Yuval was short and slim, Boaz was considerably taller and filled out. He looked like he worked out. I imagined them both at High School. Yuval, the class grass ass licking the teacher, Boaz, the football captain, a blonde on each shoulder. With the exception of the incident at Moshave Sade when he refused to see us following Stuart's suicide, he dealt with us with respect. Admittedly we did not see him nearly as often as we saw Yuval but our dealings with him were more cordial. He knew we were older, and a little life wiser, and much of the bullshit used on the young Israelis wouldn't wash with us. Before the previous trip to Lebanon he gathered the troops together, only our unit, and explained the reasoning for the action. He didn't have to do that. An order is an order and we were expected to follow whatever our political views may have been but he felt the need to respect us and explain the reasoning behind the upcoming action.

There was one occasion when we agreed as an entire unit that Yuval was detrimental to our success as a competent fighting force. Several of us, a delegation if you like, met with Boaz in his office and expressed our concerns. This was not a mutiny, not yet anyway, just a 'clearing of the air, an expression of our views and feelings'. Boaz was non-committal, he couldn't sack an officer because his soldiers didn't like him, but it was obvious Boaz didn't like him either. It was more what Boaz didn't say than what he did. At no point did he defend Yuval. Boaz hinted that soon Yuval would not be a problem for us any longer. As it turned out Boaz departed the platoon before Yuval. I often wonder what happened to Boaz, how he got on later in life. Maybe a career soldier or corporate management. Without a surname and with the long passage of time I doubt I will find out. That is a shame because he was a decent guy.

Danny played the army with finesse and guile. He went through a scam marriage before the army in order to reduce his service to just one year. He had seen his wife just once, at the wedding, but so convincing were his tales of marriage misfortunes, even the few of us that knew his secret actually believed his stories. On returning from each leave he had related tales of his wife's latest domestic disaster. He even blamed the wife for a scruffy uniform claiming she used the wrong washing detergent. The woman couldn't cook or clean principally because she didn't exist. The army rule that no soldier may spend more than three weeks on base without a weekend home was exploited beautifully by Danny. Due home one weekend after two weeks in the platoon prepared with usual excitement, except Danny who wanted the following weekend off to attend his kibbutz party. For the whole week

Danny disobeyed orders, from refusing to get out of bed each morning to sloppy behaviour on parade. True to form Danny was kept back as we departed giving him the following weekend to attend the kibbutz Purim party.

March 9th 1985 Letter to Freda

Dear Freda, Sorry, I got your letter last week but have had no time to sit and write. Everyone around me is sleeping. The generator has just turned itself off leaving the snores of my neighbour as my background music. I don't think anyone got up for guard duty last night, instead we just stayed in bed and threw rocks at the next guard who in turn threw rocks at his replacement. It was quite well organised and very funny. I am waiting for my ulpan to come through, it is in Haifa and with much better conditions. I get out every weekend. Last weekend we were on the Golan training, shit it was cold. We hiked to an old Crusader castle which was near death. You could see the whole valley and the lights of Kiryat Shmona. I remember reading Elli Cohen spy story when he stood on the Syrian side of the Golan looking towards his home and how lonely he felt. I tried to get a couple of days leave while there but no chance. Todd got back from the states today and will come back to base on Sunday.

I've just seen a mouse on my bag, it was real cute. I got a pet now. Last night regular soldiers and officers all ate together, it was a nice atmosphere. On the bus down from the Golan I supplied the music so we had five hours of Bowie, Floyd and more decent tunes.

I am still not doing training, Yuval is determined to punish me but everyone else finds it quite amusing. Seems like army attitude is not how brave you are but how much you managed to skive during your service.

Got some English tea bags so I think it's time for a cuppa. You have probably noticed from the tone of this letter that I am in a good mood at the moment. I have ups and downs but I'm gonna finish this army shit. This is the most important thing I have ever done.

Take Care, see you soon

Love Johnny.

I don't remember the exact point in the army that our personalities changed so drastically. The army attempted to carve us into a fit, lean, fighting machine. They emptied our heads of rational thought, any freedom of thought and turned us into instinctive warriors. You had to be capable of making an instant decision whether to shoot or not when confronted with the enemy. If you stood there for twenty minutes debating the issues in your head, you were dead before reaching a conclusion. Dissent was deadly. Personally we changed too. We become ultra selfish, liars and thieves. You pretended to not hear a call for help unless you deemed it serious, and your definition of serious could differ greatly from others. You would rather the platoon go hungry as you joined the long list of soldiers faking diarrhoea rather than join the kitchen crew. While your own equipment inspection failures couldn't be blamed on anybody else, communal area inspection failures were blamed on everybody else. When the tent or showers failed inspection you maintained to the inspecting officer that you did your job, it was everybody else that failed the task.

Any equipment lying unattended was 'reclaimed' by the finding soldier whether it was needed or not, whether it was labelled with the soldiers name or not. Uniforms were gold dust. An errant shirt or trousers, whatever the size, were scooped up and stuffed in your kitbag for future use. When I finally finished the army and handed back my equipment I had a surplus of an army coat, two shirts and two pairs of pants all acquired due to the negligence of some other soldier. Guaranteed he was not short either as he would have 'reclaimed' the equipment from somebody else.

We became violent. You had to push, to scrum for that second chicken leg. For us Brits it was not that easy. Israelis didn't queue, Israeli soldiers didn't even pretend to queue. When fifty soldiers were waiting for ten seats on a bus home there was no place for British reserve. You pushed, you dug your gun into the back of the soldier in front, you clipped the ankles of the soldier at the side with your bag. I had never been violent. I never engaged in the English Friday night sport of ten pints, a kebab and a fight. I was only ever in one real fight, as a teenager, and lost. I decided fighting was not for me. I wasn't very good at it. As for petty fighting, pushing, jostling, I was becoming as good as any Israeli.

I was brought up in England with a good moral code. I was taught to respect others and the law. We followed the code 'do unto others as they would do to you' amongst other rules. We followed the ten commandments, as much because they related to human decency as to obey Jewish law. The only times I had been in a police station had been to reclaim a stolen bicycle and to enlist as a police officer aged twelve. While I was not too happy at my changing personality. I hoped it was only temporary as the best way of surviving this hell.

I wasn't sure if it was the three consecutive wins by City, the return of Todd, the return of Ian and Moshe from officers course or the determination that I would not let Yuval break me but I decided to take a positive approach. Many of us, myself included, realised we were not destined to be distinguished soldiers. We were not heading for any commando course. When we had joined up some eight months earlier we had joked of becoming the greatest ever army unit but really we knew average would do fine. In reality we struggled to reach that. Now survival would do. Myself and Ian applied for the army ulpan course in Haifa. We bypassed Yuval requesting a meeting with the rarely seen Boaz. We argued that by improving our knowledge of the language we could train better. We threw quite a few English words in to the conversation to enforce our argument. It worked. I would have loved to had been a mosquito on the wall when Boaz told him two of his whipping boys were off for a months 'holiday' to Haifa.

Chapter 20 Weekend Soldier

March 24<sup>th</sup> 1985

Haifa was the largest city in northern Israel, and the third largest city in the country, with a population of over 270,000. Another 300,000 people live in towns and and some kibbutzim. It was also home to the Bahá'í World Centre, a UNESCO World Heritage Site and destination for Baha'i pilgrims. Built on the slopes of Mount Carmel, the history of settlement at the site spans more than 3,000 years. The earliest known settlement in the vicinity was Tell Abu Hawam, a small port city established in the Late Bronze Age 14th century BC. In the 3rd century CE, Haifa was known as a dye-making centre. Over the centuries, the city has changed hands: It has been conquered and ruled by many including the Persians, Romans, Byzantines, Arabs, Crusaders, Ottomans, British, and the Israelis. Since the establishment of the State of Israel in 1948, the city has been governed by the Haifa Municipality.

The city was a major seaport located on Israel's Mediterranean coastline in the Bay of Haifa. It was located about 90 kilometres north of Tel Aviv and the major regional centre of northern Israel. Two respected academic institutions, the University of Haifa and the Technion, were located in Haifa; The city played an important role in Israel's economy, home to Matam, one of the oldest and largest high-tech parks in the country. Haifa Bay was a centre of heavy industry, petroleum refining and chemical processing. Haifa was formerly the western terminus of an oil pipeline from Iraq via Jordan. After the establishment of the State of Israel Haifa became the gateway for Jewish immigration into Israel. During the 1948 Arab–Israeli War, the neighbourhoods of Haifa were sometimes contested. After the war, Jewish immigrants were settled in new neighbourhoods. As Tel Aviv gained in status, Haifa suffered a decline in the role as regional capital. The opening of Ashdod as a port exacerbated this. Tourism shrank when the Israeli Ministry of Tourism placed emphasis on developing Tiberias as a tourist centre. Nevertheless, Haifa's population had reached 200,000 by the early 1970s, and mass immigration from the former Soviet Union boosted the population by a further 35,000. Haifa is commonly portrayed as a model of coexistence between Arabs and Jews, although tensions and hostility do still exist. Jews comprise some 82% of the population, some 4% are Muslims and almost 14% are Christians, the majority of whom are Arab Christians. Haifa also includes Druze and Bahá'í.

The army ulpan base was situated on the top of Mount Carmel minutes walk from the city centre in Haifa. The soldier guard at the blue gated entrance the only clue this was an army base. Maybe the army had run out of green paint. It looked like an ordinary school. The building was separated into two sections, present and future soldiers.. New immigrants yet to be enrolled into the army and ourselves, already soldiers. There were even half a dozen Israelis with us who claimed they couldn't read or write. The army supported the education of Israelis who, for whatever reason had failed at school. While many were genuine cases, one or two of the Israelis with us, while supposedly struggling to read Hebrew in class, managed rather well in the towns pubs. While the pre-army students got a taste of the army with inspections and drilling, we were pretty much free after lessons to watch television or even leave the base. We had an evening roll call and a nightly curfew. Once the roll call had finished we could leave the base for the evening, nobody ever checked us back after the curfew. The guards, usually the not yet drafted soldiers, were too intimidated by us to question our comings and goings. Of the five weekends of the course we were required to stay back just one weekend. That weekend was decided for us following our court-martial for spending one evening in a local bar. We had spent most nights of the previous three weeks in the bar. Perhaps it was a blessing in disguise as we were by now spent up. Haifa was a popular port for the U.S. Navy and we often endured drinking sessions with the American sailors. It wasn't cheap living the high life in the army. I was almost broke, Ian was in a worse position. Our supposed weekly room inspections mostly never happened and when they did go ahead were rarely observed. The officers just went through the motions. We never really cleaned and they never really checked. The lessons were a little useful but really the best way of learning any language is to be out and around the natives.

The history of the Hebrew language is usually divided into four major periods: Biblical Hebrew, until about the 3rd century BC, in which most of the Hebrew Bible is written; Mishnaic Hebrew, the language of the Mishnah and Talmud; Medieval Hebrew, from about the 6th to the 13th century CE, and Modern Hebrew, the language of the modern State of Israel. Jewish contemporary sources describe Hebrew flourishing as a spoken language in the kingdoms of Israel and Judah, during about 1200 to about 580 BC. Derived from a biblical language, Ivrit left huge gaps in the dictionary especially with anything invented after biblical days. Helicopter in Hebrew became 'elicopter' while television became a 'televisia'.I loved the lack of imagination. Latin, Greek, even English words had complex origins while modern Hebrew words just pinched the English version. Hebrew slang was more imaginative.My favourite word was 'ze' meaning 'that or this'. Ze was the perfect bluff if you didn't know the correct word in Hebrew. If you didn't know a particular word, by using the term 'ze' and pointing at the item sometimes you could bluff your lack of knowledge.

Army slang was often language used in every day civilian life, it was as important to learn the street language as the official tongue. Gazlan, 'to rip-off;' Ice-Cream van.No matter where military exercises are located, a gazlan can always be counted upon to come rolling up ready and willing to sell ice-cream and soft-drinks to desperate soldiers for exorbitant prices. Ahabal, idiot or dumbass. comes from Arabic, as do most of the curses in Hebrew slang. Ben-zona, Son of a whore is used as a common insult, the Israeli equivalent of 'son of a bitch' or to express how awesome something is. Dafook Idiot, is one of several words that all describe, more or less, a moron.It also comes from the word 'fuck' and can be used to either describe a person or an item, for example a car that will not run as 'fucked'. The Hebrew word 'dofek' means 'bang' and again can be used to bang a nail or as sexual intercourse. Rosh katan 'Small head;' a person that shows no initiative and does only what is absolutely necessary. The opposite of the Rosh Katan is the Rosh Gadol, the 'big head,' someone who takes initiative and goes above and beyond the call of duty. While acting like a Rosh Gadol may sound commendable, in the army soldiers can be criticised for following either approach. Taking the initiative is not always the way to win acclaim with your peers in an army or civilian institution run by twenty year old commanders or young managers insecure about their own authority and decision making. One phrase often said to me was 'Tzavta' meaning grandmother. Shortened from 'tell your grandmother' it is used when somebody is droning on boring the listener. 'You are boring, go tell your grandmother, she may be interested'.

The ulpan on kibbutz and in the army may have taught us the basics of the language, the structure of Hebrew grammar, verbs and the like but it was our interaction with Israelis where we learned the real language. Our time in Haifa had been a blast. We had drank ourselves silly, avoided the heat and cold of the most inhospitable corners of Israel and, most importantly, chalked another six weeks off our army service. The ulpan was drawing to the end and it was time for stage two of the master plan. I was in no mood for returning to Yuvals army. A masterplan was necessary. Ian wrote me a letter to hand into the ulpan commander. A compassionate and sad letter supposedly from my father explaining the separation of my parents. Of course I was devastated. I would be needed back home at this time of need. I applied for compassionate leave to England. The officer fought back the tears as he signed the papers. He offered his best wishes as I fought back the laughter. My parents marriage was really in considerably better shape than City's promotion push. Defeat to Notts County left the blues with needing victory against Charlton on the last game of the season. To add insult to injury United had reached the FA Cup final against Everton. It was strange visiting England. I could never consider staying. This wasn't home anymore. My few friends were gone and besides spending time with family there were few memorable moments. Often I felt like an outsider.


Chapter 21 Old England

May 11th 1985

I tried, god did I try but 42,285 City fans got their tickets for Maine Road before I could and I resorted to listening to the game on the radio. Anything but a city win would give

Portsmouth promotion. Not a second season fourth, please. From the start we pounded the Charlton defences. It was like Garin Nesher on manoeuvres, the precision of their attacks, their tactical ability, not. By 4.45pm Philips with two goals plus May, Simpson and Melrose we were back in the top flight. Charlton pulled a goal back but it was too late by then. Having experienced the traumas of the season from behind a sand dune some two thousand miles away most of the season it was fitting I was back in Manchester for this momentous day.

## May 18th 1985 Wembley Blues

Continuing the football journey, my father had obtained cup final tickets. Myself and brother Paul took the train with hundreds of United fans down to Wembley. Our true identities, we were blues, we kept secret. I hadn't yet trained as a spy but this was good practice. From the perceptive of a city fan Norman Whiteside ruined my day by scoring the only goal in a united victory. If nothing else the visit back to England reinforced the fact that my childhood was over and it was time to finally grow up. Walking through Broughton Park reminded me of my days of innocence, now long gone. The bike rides around Spring Vale, football in the park with Simon. Shit he always kicked the ball so hard when I was in goal. He would always apologise by giving me a great diving shot to save. Two trees served as goalposts, a park bench behind the goals on the path served as the stands. Two young lovers who often sat on the bench holding hands were our regular crowd though in truth I'm not sure they ever paid any attention to us. We would spend hours, just the two of us, as dusk set in and we would retreat to his house to hang out. At Simon's we could devour endless bars of chocolate and more importantly smoke in the bedroom without parental scorn.

We thought we were so clever leading a Zionist youth group preaching years of Israeli propaganda. It had taken the army to show me much of the real Israel, to distinguish the truth from the bullshit. Much of what we preached was true and factual but a lot was just complete bollocks. We had done mostly good work bringing Israel to the Jewish youth of Manchester. At sixteen and seventeen years old we had run an organisation, a charity with a budget of thousands of pounds.We had organised charity fund raising events, weekend seminars and cultural lectures. We did well really even if I did end with a nervous breakdown and had neglected my school studies.

Broughton Park was quiet, it always was. The ducks waddled around the empty children s playground before flying back to the lake.It was pleasant and warm, not the humid Israeli heat. The sun lowered behind the distant trees before hitting the calm lake. I sat by my favourite tree for a short while. I lit a cigarette flicking the spent match into the distance. I took slow drags blowing the smoke into the still air. Nobody passed and I enjoyed the quiet and solitude. I thought too much, that was my problem. Everything had to be analysed. There had to be a reason for everything, every question required an answer. I hated the army. It was hard and painful. I wanted it over but I wasn't sorry I had enlisted. I didn't feel the pride I had been expecting, maybe I would after it was all over? I could look back and remember only the good times, there had been a few. I missed my friends. I missed Jo and Todd, Ian and Jeremy. Simon, Dave, Elyse were my past, my new friends were my future. I had to stay strong for them, they had to do the same for me. We would never survive without each other, Stuart had sadly shown that.

My first year as an Israeli citizen. I had made the move so many had dreamed of, millions had prayed for, millions had died for. There were those like Simon and Dave that had no interest in Israel and I understood and respected that. Others that thought a two week holiday at the Tel Aviv Hilton and an annual donation to plant a few trees in a Jerusalem forest made them Israeli. The purchase of a few Jaffa oranges does not buy you citizenship, especially when it was me putting my safety on the line to protect a state that, should things all go tits up in Europe, would provide a safe haven for them in Israel. Yes sometimes I felt aloof, arrogant even. I understood a lot of the arrogance of Israelis. I was often treated like a war hero on my return to England. It was hugely satisfying to enter a room with my father who, with a huge smile on his face, introduced me to strangers as his son, an Israeli soldier. No I wasn't an exemplary soldier by any means, but I was doing more than the diaspora Jews were. Israel was not the country portrayed by the Zionist organisations but it was a good country, faults like any other place. I was really becoming an Israeli. I had gone there to live the Jewish dream, fulfil the dream of 2000 years, but now I felt different. I wasn't there for the religion. I just loved the place, its physical beauty and its crazy people. I loved my friends. Israel was the name I first looked out for during the football world cup draw or Eurovision song contest. Israel was my home.

Of course I missed my family and my football, it was awful in Israel, but I needed more than Saturday night coffee in the Midland Hotel. I had found myself and people with similar interests and goals. That isn't to say mine were better, just different. I wasn't hiding anymore, least of all behind the football pink.As I watched the squabbling ducks from under my oak tree I missed the kibbutz air filled with BBQ smoke and laughter.

Chapter 22 To The Morning

May 27th 1985

On my return to my unit I noticed a whole host of changes. Yuval had departed. Nobody knew if he jumped or was pushed but either way he was gone without a tear shed. I was looking forward to a new, positive start. Jeremy, while visiting his family back in America was involved in a serious motorbike accident and was recovering in hospital. Danny had been discharged having served his mandatory year while Malcolm joined Andy and Dave in lowering their medical profiles and joining Peter and the girls on an army base that would later become a kibbutz. I imagined Malcolm's horror on arriving at the Echzut to join the others and meet his new commander...... Yuval.

All that remained were myself, Moshe and Ian. The remainder of the platoon had moved on to paratroopers course. And Todd. Todd now returned to the states leaving us another man down but more importantly one big friend down. Todd seemed to have suffered more than most others especially after Stuart's suicide and his well built, tough exterior beguiled a sensitive interior. This was not the Israel we had envisaged. I had grown close to Todd, closer to him than any of the others in the garin. We had shared secrets without fear of recrimination. He was my confidant on the kibbutz and I felt lost without him. As the garin fractured Peter and Jo felt the loss of Todd too. Peter seemed to distance himself from the group. Myself and Jo were feeling more and more alienated in the garin and on the kibbutz. We were becoming much closer friends. Less than a year previously we were thirty new immigrants bonded together to shine in our army training and move on to paratroopers unit. Now we were just three, the remainder scattered throughout the army or out of the country. We were pathetic in truth.

While the name Garin Nesher sent a cold shiver around Nahal General HQ we were hardly flavour of the month on Kfar Blum either. Tongues were wagging and we were seen more of a burden and embarrassment to the kibbutz. Following Stuart's suicide, Todd's departure and several indiscretions on our part an article in the kibbutz newspaper called for our expulsion. Tensions between the garin and kibbutz grew. Pre-army promises from both sides were reneged upon. Jo, Janet and Yaffa all requested a transfer to another kibbutz but the army refused. Infighting within the garin took hold. Most of us, myself included, spent as little time as possible on the kibbutz. Our free weekends from the army were almost always spent elsewhere. Our differences were pretty much insurmountable.If the garin was our family, we were a family at war, completely dysfunctional.

August 16th 1985

Guess That's Why They Call It The Blues

It was a fond farewell to Ruth at the airport after a summer of screwing and swimming in the River Jordan. Obviously my visits home were short and infrequent, and often when I was back, I was fit for little. That said, I would try my upmost to perform my required duties. We had a good time together when her soldier returned from the war. She had spent some of the summer as one of three councillors on an American Jewish youth programme. One activity included a weekend in Eilat and lunch on a boat out in the Red Sea. I had a long weekend off from the army and I joined the group. The councillors added a few dollars to the trip price to the students to cover my costs. As a special treat myself and Ruth got the double room for ourselves, the two other selfless councillors sharing for the weekend.

I had travelled with Ruth and the group in my army uniform. I had come straight from the base meeting the group in Tel Aviv before travelling south to Eilat. Ruth had collected some civilian clothes for me from the kibbutz. In truth I could have changed clothes in the toilets before travelling but I enjoyed impressing the young American kids as a soldier. I think also Ruth liked showing off her soldier hero boyfriend.

Israelis have a worldwide reputation for being blunt and arrogant. That said they look after their own, we look after own own. Many cafes and restaurants around the country display two price menus, one for civilians and discounts for soldiers. I have lost count of the occasions I have bought a felafel whilst in uniform and the vendor has thrown me a free can of coke. Every leave I had from the army I had at least half a dozen places to stay with friends. It was not unusual to see a soldier carrying his bag and gun home on a weekend leave, walking through the market in Tel Aviv, Jerusalem or wherever, and see a trader toss the soldier an apple or bagel. Everybody is a soldier here. The market stall holder giving the apple to the soldier has a son himself who is a soldier, the stall holder was a soldier himself. This probably more than anything else is what makes Israel so beautiful.

Ruth still had a lot of friends on the kibbutz so wasn't too bored while I was away defending the nation. We had a song now, corny I know. Elton John 'Guess that's why they call it the blues'. I would miss her not being there when I returned from the base. I was going to get high and chill, drown my lonely sorrows out the weekend when Marc and Stephen made a surprise visit to the kibbutz. We had been together during Year Course. I had tried to keep in touch with many from Year Course, they were good people. We had kept in touch throughout the years. Stephen had just joined the army in the Golani Brigade. He reminded me of Todd, well built and physically strong. A friend that would back you until the end. Golani was a lot tougher than Nahal, whatever Nahal soldiers may say. I hoped he would cope. We stood together in our Israeli army uniforms and took photographs. I felt good for the first time in a while. Five years ago we were two eighteen year old Jewish kids full of the Zionist ideal. We pledged to return to Israel after the course, to serve in the army and make our lives in the holy land. And here we were doing just that. Meeting up with Stephen, and Marc, gave me added purpose. I hadn't been too good a soldier so far, I wanted to be good, or at least the best I could be. Yes I had been held back by Yuval but I couldn't put every shortcoming down to him. With Yuval gone and seeing Stephen in uniform and doing well, I was ready for a new start.

Jewish New Year and a real downer. The dining room was filled with soldiers relaxing and singing while I sat outside alone. I was missing my family back in England. Although I hated visiting the synagogue as a teenager and avoided it when older, and I was no great fan of religion in general, I did enjoy a lot of the tradition. It seemed to be much like the Christian celebration of Christmas, a huge build up to the day, followed by a huge fight at dinner time. The only real difference was that Jews managed to cause a riot without alcohol. There was a lot to be said for tradition. I missed my grandmothers chopped liver and meat balls. I missed my mothers chicken soup. As I sat on the base I even missed the three hours sitting in the synagogue. It was hard to believe but I had served 412 days in the army. I would be happy on my 550$^{th}$ day, my last day.

Chapter 23 Redemption Song
October 1st 1985

Desert Song
In this desert of dreams
Sandstorms cover my tracks
The burning sun brings me to my knees
There's no turning back
Your friendship guides me onwards
My feet blistered in the sand
Only the sun to guide me
This is not what was planned
One step at a time now
Your vision in my head
Your words, a well of sweet water
I treasure every word you said
I will meet you in the morning
We will start over again
Your voice in the desert stars
Will take away the pain
In this desert of dreams
A single palm stands proud and tall
It's shelter, your love, A lesson to us all.

My second birthday in uniform with just Ian and Moshe to help me celebrate, or at least I thought so. My army service changed remarkably within the new Israeli platoon. Myself, Ian and Moshe were treated with much respect by our younger colleagues and officers. There was no melted Mars bar this birthday but the Israelis around us tried their best to make my day as bearable as possible. The young Israelis were genuinely fascinated by our decision to leave the comforts of abroad to stumble over a desert wasteland miles away. They respected our motivation if not our realism. That respect was easily reciprocated. The training we had missed due to Yuvals restrictions made no difference as our new officer offered extra tuition and encouragement. My Hebrew improved remarkably once I was given the support. I was now beginning to enjoy my service. I had, after all, joined to train and be able, if needed, to defend my country. I was happy to achieve that. Yossi, my new officer offered me the radio. At first I handed it back expressing my fears that my inexperience could put the rest of my comrades in danger. Yossi ignored my claims and within a short time I was familiar with the codes, the correct procedure and filled with the confidence Yuval had robbed from me. By halting our training Yuval had made certain we would not pass the required level of 'Rifle 3' to continue our combat training. Yossi, our new officer was shocked and disgusted. Under army regulations we should have been returned to Base 80 to retake basic training. Instead Yossi personally brought us up to the required level. To this day my army records show I never passed basic training. It was ironic that I joined a platoon of new immigrants to help me through the army yet it was a bunch of Israeli kids that helped me prove my worth as a soldier.

Now the training was both worthwhile and enjoyable. The huge training exercise with almost half the entire Israeli army taking part was awesome and I felt a part of it. We used live ammunition attacking mock enemy positions with artillery cover, tanks and even air cover. This was serious playing soldiers. Climbing hills, diving into trenches and crawling through thorn bushes, while tough, now had a purpose. With the huge radio strapped to my back I felt little of the extra weight as we charged the lines. The contrast was stark. We had done the same exercise previously with Yuval and Boaz commanding us. It was now clear they had deliberately given us a benign role.On this exercise we were in the forefront of the exercise, involved, active and highly competent. Finally, a year late, I was a soldier. It was a good feeling.

As it happened one Israeli garin serving with us were based at Kibbutz Shamir which neighboured Kfar Blum, our home. We travelled back to the north together laughing as we had done over a year ago on those first few journeys back home. The soldiers from Shamir invited myself and Moshe to a steak dinner on our arrival at Kiryat Shmona to celebrate my birthday. Seven of us sat at the long table outside the bar. The table was crammed with salads, plates of humus, olives, pickles, pita breads and enormous steaks. We ate like royalty. The beer and laughter flowed. We sat for a few hours. If the Israelis were eager to get home to their loved ones they never showed it. When the bill arrived they would not let me contribute towards the bill. They were the reason we were putting ourselves through the shit of the army. They showed how a garin could be cohesive and bond well. They put Garin Nesher to shame.

Meanwhile as I prospered, the same couldn't be said for my beloved Manchester City. Just two victories in eleven games

144

including a 3-0 hammering by United at Maine Road. It looked like we were doomed to return to the second division. The new season back in Division One began with an average start with two draws and a loss but was followed by two wins over West Brom and Spurs. The slide followed with losses to Birmingham, Southampton, Oxford, Chelsea, Watford and the killer, a battering by United at home.It seemed that the easier the army got for myself, the more difficult the football season became for the blues.

There seemed little point in spending my weekends at Kfar Blum. Jo spent most weekends with her family and boyfriend in Tel Aviv. Janet and Yaffa weren't talking to me after I voted against them a few months earlier over one Garin issue. Jeff did return but spent all of his time with his kibbutz girlfriend, as did Malcolm. There was only really Moshe and honestly after an hour in his company the rope at the River Jordan became a real attraction. Annette and Steven, my kibbutz family were supportive and welcoming but it wasn't enough to draw me to the kibbutz too often. It didn't help that we were not too popular amongst the members. Any time we spent with the volunteers we were alcoholic louts, any time with the American Class we were perverts. We were supposedly prospective members yet denied any privileges like using the kibbutz cars. There was no real reason to visit. Instead I would visit Tzuba and Stella much more often.

With my sisters wedding coming up it was time to take my second trip back to England, this time with a little sadness. My last visit to England had been to escape the army. I felt differently now. I was doing well and happy, well as happy as you could be in the army. I bid farewell to my fellow soldiers and as I departed I was actually looking forward to my return.

Chapter 24 A New England

November 16th 1985

My three weeks in England passed a great deal faster than I had expected. While my visit the previous year had been a little tedious at times, this visit was far more enjoyable. Suzanne's wedding, a lavish affair, took up much of my time. My reservations about wearing a dinner suit were ignored. I had forgotten about dinner suits and vol-au-vents. I was an Israeli now, a war hero and we only wore bow ties under protest. The overly camp fitter at the suit hire shop was far from impressed with my lack of enthusiasm and sarcasm. Posh Jewish 'Simchas, celebrations' were a norm for me just a few years before but they didn't seem the Israeli way. I was wrong, some Israeli events were on a huge, expensive and overly lavish affair, even bigger than some in England. I just never moved in those circles.

One pleasant surprise for myself and family was the visit of Ruth from America. In reality our long distance relationship was on the wane and my feeble attempts at fidelity had failed miserably, still it was good to see her. Speculation amongst the wedding guests was rife that we would announce a double wedding. I let the rumour persist, it was more fun that way. While we enjoyed the time together, including an episode in a town centre car park, it seemed clear to me we would probably not be together in the summer when she would return to Israel. I particularly enjoyed the debate between my parents as Ruths sleeping arrangements were discussed. My father had no objection to her sharing my room while my mother flitted between shock and horror.

'Nita, really, what do you think they did in Israel?' my father asked my mother.

On my last visit I had felt a little like a fraud, treated as a war hero, I had done little more than guard an ammunition dump. Admittedly this hadn't been all my fault but still I felt a little uneasy with the praise heaped upon me. Now I felt different. I was an integral part of my unit serving as effectively as my fellow soldiers. I accepted the praise more comfortably. Simon and Dave were around for the wedding and after Ruth left to join her mother in London I met up with Simon. For old times sake we spent a little time in Broughton Park where he kicked a football very hard and I burned my hands trying to stop it. We also put ourselves through a painful one all draw at Maine Road as we joined twenty thousand other fans watch Ipswich Town hold city to a tedious draw. In the cold November, Manchester air, I realised I wasn't missing too much of England. I was excited to return home.

## Chapter 25 The Lebanon

The 1982 Lebanon war, called Operation Peace for Galilee began on June 6th 1982 when the Israeli Defence Forces invaded Southern Lebanon after repeated attacks and counter-attacks between the Palestinian Liberation Organisation operating in southern Lebanon and the IDF which caused civilian casualties on both sides of the border. The military operation was launched after gunmen from Abu Nidal Organisation attempted to assassinate Shlomo Argov, Israel's ambassador to the United Kingdom. Prime Minister Menachim Begin blamed the PLO, for the incident,and treated the incident as reason for the invasion. After attacking the PLO, as well as Syrian and Muslim Lebanese forces, Israeli military, in cooperation with the Maronite allies and the self-proclaimed Free Lebanon State occupied southern Lebanon, eventually surrounding the PLO and elements of the Syrian army that were helping the PLO. Surrounded in West Beirut and subjected to heavy bombardment, the PLO forces and their allies negotiated passage from Lebanon with the aid of United States and the protection of international peacekeepers. The PLO, under the chairmanship of Yasser Arafat had relocated its headquarters to Tripoli in June 1982. By expelling the PLO, removing Syrian influence over Lebanon, and installing a pro-Israeli Christian government led by Bachir Gemayel. Israel hoped to sign a treaty which Begin promised would give Israel "forty years of peace".

Following the assassination of Bachir Gemayel, Israel's position in Beirut became untenable and the signing of a peace treaty became increasingly unlikely. Outrage followed Israel turning a blind eye in the Phalangist perpetrated Sabra and Shatila massacre of mostly Palestinians and Lebanese Shiites. Israeli popular disillusionment with the war lead to a gradual withdrawal from Beirut to the areas claimed by the self-proclaimed Free Lebanon State in southern Lebanon. After Israeli forces withdrew from most of Lebanon, war in the refugee camps broke out between Lebanese factions, the remains of PLO and Syria, in which Syria fought its former Palestinian allies. At the same time, Shia militant groups began consolidating and waging a terrorist campaign against the Israeli occupation of southern Lebanon, leading to over 15 years of low scale armed conflict. In February 1985, Israel withdrew from Sidon and turned it over to the Lebanese Army, but faced attacks: 15 Israelis were killed and 105 wounded during the withdrawal. Dozens of SLA members were also assassinated. From mid-February to mid-March, Israel lost 18 dead and 35 wounded. On 11 March, Israeli forces raided the town of Zrariyah, killing forty fighters and capturing a large stock of arms. On 9 April, a Shiite girl drove a car bomb into an IDF convoy, and the following day, a soldier was killed by a land mine. During that same period, Israeli forces killed 80 Lebanese terrorists in five weeks. Israel withdrew from the Bekaa valley on 24 April, and from Tyre on the 29th, but continued to occupy a security zone in Southern Lebanon.

Between 6 June 1982 and June 1985, the Israel Defence Forces suffered 657 dead and 3,887 wounded. From the withdrawal to the South Lebanon Security Zone in 1985 to the pullout to the international border in May 2000, the IDF lost another 559 soldiers, including 256 from combat. If the Lebanon war had succeeded in displacing the PLO, in the screwed up world of Middle East politics, one enemy was simply replaced by another, Hezbollah. The South Lebanon Security Belt, initially in coordination with the self-proclaimed Free Lebanon State, executed a limited authority over portions of southern Lebanon with the South Lebanon Army. Israel's stated purpose for the Security Belt was to create a space separating its northern border towns from terrorists residing in Lebanon. During the stay in the security belt, the IDF held many positions and supported the SLA. The SLA took over daily life in the security zone, initially as the official force of the Free Lebanon State and later as an allied militia. In addition, United Nations forces and the United Nations Interim Force in Lebanon (UNIFIL) were deployed to the security belt. The strip was a few miles wide, and consisted of about ten percent of the total territory of Lebanon, which housed about 150,000 people who lived in around sixty villages and towns made up of Shiites, Maronites and Druze, most of whom lived in the town of Hatzbaya, our home too. We were part of the estimated thousand Israeli troops scattered around the security zone on around twenty bases varying in size.

My ego had soared to the degree that I fully expected the red carpet and a fanfare on my return to Israel. Neither happened and instead I returned to the kibbutz for a couple of days before my return to my unit. I was shocked to find they had left the country in my absence. It was like getting home from your holiday and finding your family had moved home without telling you. They had been deployed to Lebanon and my orders were to join them as soon as possible. It was good to feel wanted. I did not relish serving over the border in a foreign land, especially with people shooting at me. On the positive side, journeys home at weekends would be considerably shorter. In true army fashion I had undergone no training, no briefing for my service in hostile territory. I don't know if my fellow soldiers had received any pre-Lebanon instruction as I had been back in England. I reported to an army base at Metulla, the crossing point into Lebanon, with all my equipment. I didn't need my passport or visa as invading forces are apparently exempt. I was told which convoy to join by a clerk in the office. A jobnik was sending me to battle, to a war zone, to possible death. I was a little bemused and hurt that someone more senior wasn't there to oversee such a momentous occasion. And what of the practical? What if we were ambushed? Did the jobnik clerk know I would be able to perform? Did the army have complete faith in my ability? No, that didn't matter. What was important to the army was I was a body, a number. I didn't understand it at all. I worked in England in retail. You don't employ somebody until you have checked their references, interviewed them or actually seen their work. How do you send someone to war without checking them out first. I guessed that even if I had stood in the office pointing my gun the wrong way round or with my underwear on my head they still would have sent me. As with the incident with medics course, it doesn't matter the quality of the soldiers, the number is key.

They say the older you get the more right wing politically you become. It seemed for us the exception proved the rule. Perhaps our more western background made us left wing as such. It may be easier calling for peace and coexistence when you are two thousand miles away from exploding buses. The young Israelis were mostly at best ambivalent to the Arabs, at worst openly hostile. I really wasn't completely comfortable at being part of an occupying force in another country. The Occupied Territories of Gaza and The West Bank were one thing. They could be very loosely be termed part of Israel but Lebanon really was a separate country. We were defending our country from infiltrating terrorists. We were policing a buffer zone between Hezbollah terrorists and Israeli citizens, a job the United Nations peacekeepers were failing to do, but we were still occupying a foreign sovereign state. The young Israelis serving with us saw no problem with this. We were told this was something we had to do and mostly accepted that. All that said, it was exciting. A tale for the grandchildren maybe.

In many ways the Israeli war in Lebanon in 1982 was Israel's Vietnam. Many books and movies have been made eulogising the small nation that overcame the mighty evil neighbouring aggressors. Israel was the David against Goliath. By the 1980s Israel was now, in the worlds eyes, the Goliath. The poor little Palestinians were now the wronged people. Unfortunately there is no grey in the Middle East, just black and white. In previous wars Israeli soldiers returned home to a heroes welcome. Following the Lebanon war soldiers returned to Tel Aviv to be met by Peace Now activists waving banners accusing the soldiers of being child killers. Israel's most famous author Amos Oz describes in a 1982 essay 'the tear that Prime Minister Menachem Begin is making in the fabric of our national consensus of many decades - a consensus by which we launched a full-scale war only when our very existence was in danger.' It is this assault on the national consensus that is the cardinal sin, and the responsibility lies squarely with Begin. As Amos Oz put it, 'I do not understand the tendency of many mainstream Labour party people these days to assign the responsibility for this war to Ariel Sharon and Rafael Eitan, and to depict Begin as being led, without a mind of his own, by these two. On the contrary: Sharon is a clumsy but obedient instrument.'

Si Himan, a popular pop singer sang a couple of years later 'From Tel Aviv to Beirut, I fear who will die from some stupidity' and in the song 'Big Hero' she sang sarcastically 'Wars don't happen in Winter, it's too cold to conquer, wars don't happen in Summer, it's too hot to hate'. So polarised was the country that while the audience inside her concerts cheered the artist and her sentiments, demonstrators outside pelted eggs at the artist. In 1986 the movie Shtei Etzbaot Mi'Tzidon, Two Fingers from Sidon was released. The story of a platoon of Israeli soldiers in Lebanon of 1986, shortly before Israeli withdrawal, and the dilemmas they faced in having to fight against Lebanese fighters in a hostile but civilian area. The film was meant to be provocative, to lead to discussions, and to raise some of the moral quandaries encountered by soldiers on a battlefield crowded with civilians and enemies as clearly differentiated as two shades of gray. Because the movie was intended to be shown only to soldiers, the army leadership allowed the three writers and the director to explore, with a $100,000 army budget, very sensitive issues, such as battle fatigue, the accidental killing of innocent civilians by Israeli troops, and the view by most Israeli soldiers at the end of the occupation that the war was utterly absurd. The result was a ninety minute training film, 'Two Fingers From Sidon,' that had one big problem, it was too good.

Israel has always been a country of paradoxes, but this one surely ranks with the best of them: a highly critical feature movie produced by the Israeli Army about a war it conducted, using actors who were serving in the army, and primarily filmed on location in the last month of the real full-scale Israeli occupation of Lebanon. On top of that, a local Lebanese village drama group, under real occupation, played the parts of the Lebanese civilians and terrorists while the infantry unit assigned to protect the film makers on location served as extras.To appreciate how extraordinary it is that the Israeli Army Film Unit should have produced this feature drama, consider an early scene. Gadi, a young, new officer, arrives at an infantry post in southern Lebanon, goes into the kitchen and meets Georgie, a veteran of the Lebanon occupation.

'Seriously, what's going on here?' Gadi asks. 'I'll give you the lowdown on it,' says Georgie, stirring a pot of onions. 'Actually, I didn't know what was going on until yesterday. They brought us some Ph.D. - an Orientalist and he gave us a lecture about the lay of the land. Now I see the light. Well, this is the way it goes. The Christians hate the Druse, and the Shiites, the Sunnis and the Palestinians, too. The Druse hate the Christians. No . . . yes . . . O.K., the Druse hate the Christians, the Shiites and the Syrians. Why? The Shiites, they've been shafted for ages so they hate them all. The Sunnis hate whoever their boss tells them to hate, and the Palestinians hate one another in addition to all the other factions.'

Then Georgie concludes: 'Now, there's one common denominator. All of them together hate - and, oh boy, how they hate - us, the Israelis.

In early 1985, Mr. Cohen presented a treatment and then a script to the Chief of Staff for approval. The army brass took until April 30, 1985, but finally approved it with only a few minor changes. By this time, however, the army had been ordered to pull out almost entirely from Lebanon and the film unit had exactly 12 days to shoot on location before they, too, had to withdraw. Most of the generals who viewed the film approved it enthusiastically, and, after considering the matter for several weeks, the Chief of Staff agreed to let it be released to the public.

In 1973, the last 'major' Arab-Israeli war Israel was just twenty five years old, a young, immature, juvenile state. Many of its errors made on the world stage were put down to simple immaturity by the worlds onlookers. By 1982 Israel, now in its mid thirties, should know better. What may be understandable for a young, new state is not acceptable for an older, more mature country. The British Empire, the French, Dutch and Americans all had tarnished histories not to mention the Germans, Italians and Japanese but higher morals were expected from the Jews. Many Israeli soldiers who served in Lebanon feared not only attacks from Hezbollah terrorists, but also verbal and physical attacks from citizens, family and friends back home. The war, and the occupation of South Lebanon afterwards ripped apart families, friendships and relationships. It tore a huge wound into the body and soul of the country. The scars remain to this day.

We travelled as a large convoy and with typical army organization it took the best part of the day to finalise our departure. We finally moved off around 4pm, in truth far too late as the convoy would be moving through terrorist country in the dark. I hoped I would be amongst the first drops. We were two supply trucks, an armoured personnel truck escorted by two jeep's, one at the front, one at the rear. I felt important, and frightened sat up front. I fought the temptation to stand up and wave the convoy through shouting 'Waggons ahoy'. The wired gates of Metulla opened and the guard waved us through like a scene from some second rate war movie. I remembered visiting the gates, called The Good Fence on one of my previous trips to Israel. I remember the group leader explaining 'This is the border with Lebanon, The Good Fence is called so as this is where Lebanese civilians can enter Israel for work or medical treatment'. He had made it all so matter of fact and noble like any civilian could just turn up and come inside, as simple as a Brit hopping over to France. I doubted his testimony. This wasn't a simple border between two countries, not a simple border like England and France, not even a more complicated border like America and Mexico. This was a border between two nations at war. You can't just turn up and walk through, and if you could, where was the passport control? The group leader was full of propaganda, full of shit. This was a border for troops and tanks to enter another country.

The driver sped through waving back and giving him a thumbs up we sped towards the snow covered Mount Hermon in the distance. It had clearly snowed recently and although mostly clear, remnants of slush on the road splattered into the adjacent farmland. The driver said something but I couldn't hear over the screech of the tyres. I just smiled back politely. The journey took a good two hours as we weaved along the narrow, newly paved road. Say one thing for the invading Israeli army, they did provide the locals with new paved roads. We passed lush countryside much the same as the landscape on the other side of the border. There were just a few buildings along the roadside but no signs of the civil war that had ripped the country apart a few years previous. Neither were there signs of the Israeli invasion three years before.

Lebanon was beautiful. It reminded me of my infrequent visits to the Lake District in England. Rolling hills, lush green rolling hills with vibrant, healthy looking cedar trees dispersed liberally. Every few yards we passed fields of olive trees and grape vines. This was the perfect holiday destination for walkers and cyclists. This was Bronte country with bullets. Wow, if these people could get their shit together Lebanon could return to the days of the past when it was packed with French tourists. Over two decades of civil war and terror had not only deprived Lebanon of valuable tourism income, it had deprived the world of experiencing such a beautiful country. Darkness was now almost upon us and I grew impatient for our arrival at the base. The experienced driver, sensing this, began singing badly out of tune. He stopped his poor rendition of the Beatles classic 'A day in the life'

'I saw a film today, oh boy, The Israel army had just won the war, A crowd of people turned away

But I just had to look, Having read the book, I'd love to turn you on.'

I was impressed with his knowledge of English.

'Me ayfo atah?, where are you from?' he asked

'Kfar Blum' I replied

from those two words he deduced I was not Israeli born.

'England or America?' he asked in English.

'England, Manchester' I replied

'Ah, Manchester United' he laughed.

Manchester has just two claims to fame. Throughout the world it is Manchester United while in America, a country not too big on soccer, the claim is the show and film 'Hair' which features a song called 'Manchester, England'

'No Manchester City' I reply.

'They're shit aren't they' he chirps

'Yup' I reluctantly agree.

'Beautiful country eh?' says my driver.

I nod in agreement.

He takes one hand from the wheel and points into the distance. 'See those hills there, Hezbollah, behind every fucking hill, this is their fucking playground. Let them fucking keep it I say'

Everybody had an opinion and they were all correct. I didn't. I didn't know what was right and what was wrong. What I did know was this fuckers driving would probably get us before Hezbollah.

We passed through the Arab town of Hatzbaya weaving through the narrow streets. We came to a near stop as the large army vehicles negotiated the tight turns. There were no civilians about in the streets but I still felt vulnerable As we turned one corner I spotted a young child kicking a football against a shop metal shutter. He wore a Barcelona football club shirt that looked like it hadn't been washed in months. As the jeep picked up speed and whisked past him our eyes met. I saw both an innocent poor child and a terrorist. I felt compassion and fear. My heart raced. Again dubious army logic was to send the convoys on the same days at the same time. It would not be beyond even the most stupid terrorist to lay in wait for the convoy and attack. The town was deserted except for the practising Pele. The few shops and cafes were all closed. I didn't know if it was after shopping hours or if they closed for the duration of the convoy. I never heard of any incidents of Israeli soldiers stopping off at the town and rampaging. In all honesty, I think we would all be too scared to get out of our vehicles.

We finally arrived at the base near of Hatzbaya about thirty kilometres inside Lebanon. I was the only soldier getting off at this stop and was greeted by Yossi, the officer, and a few of my colleagues. It was good to be reunited. They had already been there a few weeks and were familiar with the set up and layout. Most new arrivals were given a tour of the base before settling in but in total darkness any tour was futile. I was dismissed and told to report for guard duty at 2am.


Chapter 26 Billy Don't Be A Hero

November 20th 1985

I was woken just before two o'clock ready for my guard shift. I had slept in my full uniform, even my boots. I wanted to be completely ready when attacked. There were three guards on duty at any one time. Our role was to detect any terrorist attack from the distance. How we achieved that with complete darkness around was anybody's guess.

Our enemy were Hezbollah. Hezbollah's origins and ideology stemmed from the Iranian Revolution. The revolution had called for a religious Muslim government that would represent the oppressed and downtrodden Muslims of the world as they saw it. The fact that almost all of these oppressed Muslims were victims of Muslim dictators was dismissed by the group.. According to Hezbollah, the United States were to blame for many of the country's problems. Israel was seen as an extension of the United States and a foreign power in Lebanon. The organisation itself started in 1982 as part of the Iranian government's Revolutionary Guard Corps. Led by religious clerics, the organisation wanted to adopt an Iranian doctrine as a solution to Lebanese political malaise. This doctrine included the use of terror as a means of attainting political objectives. Towards the end of 1982, Iran sent fighters to assist in the establishment of a revolutionary Islamic movement in Lebanon. Iran's hope was that the new members would participate in the Jihad, or Holy War, against Israel. These forces, which were located in the area of Ba'albek in the northern Beqa'a valley, brought Iranian Islamic influence to the area and constituted the core of the Hezbollah organization in Lebanon. Thousands of Hezbollah activists and members were located in the Beqa'a valley, Beirut and southern Lebanon. These areas also offered a base for the recruitment of additional activists and fighters among the local Shi'ite populations.

Hezbollah was believed to have kidnapped and tortured to death U.S. Army colonel William R. Higgins and the CIA Station Chief in Beirut, William Buckley, and to have kidnapped around 30 other Westerners. Hezbollah was suspected of involvement in numerous terrorist attacks. The organization was responsible for the suicide truck bombings of the U.S. Embassy and U.S. Marine barracks in Beirut in October 1983, in which 241 American servicemen were killed and the U.S. Embassy annex in Beirut in September 1984. The bombing at the Marine barracks in Beirut was the deadliest single-day death toll for the United States Marine Corps since the second World War. Three members of Hezbollah were on the FBI's list of 22 Most Wanted Terrorists for the hijacking in 1985 of TWA Flight 847 during which a U.S. Navy diver was murdered. Elements of the group were responsible for the kidnapping and detention of Americans and other westerners in Lebanon in the 1980s. Hezbollah were more than happy to carry out the dirty work of Syria, Iran and other Arab regimes by attacking Israel. There was an impasse here. The Israeli's were in South Lebanon to stop terrorists using Lebanon as a staging ground for attacks. Hezbollah were attacking because the Israeli's were there. The simple solution would have been for the Israeli's to retreat and Hezbollah to cease their rocket fire into Israel. However in the Middle East, retreat and compromise are seen as weakness and neither side was willing to show this perceived weakness. As a result, we had to sit in a tiny bunker in the Winter cold waiting for the next terrorist to play chicken with a Merkava tank.

The guard post measured just a few square feet, a metal cage not unlike the cabin of a heavy goods vehicle. Sandbags surrounded the post and protected the roof. A large machine gun directed towards barren the hills opposite. Fuck it was dark. As I entered my post the 'Ratz Lila' offered me his pearl of wisdom. 'You can't see a fucking thing but if you hear anything just shoot'. Now I felt even more scared. The 'Ratz Lila' role was to spend the night moving between the three guard posts. He would bring coffee, relieve us for toilet breaks and chat to us to keep us awake during our shift. Some even cooked a light snack. He saw how terrified I was and sat with me for about ten minutes. It was deadly quiet. A thick fog set in and now my visibility was done to about five steps. Now it was dark and foggy. In reality I was defenceless. Should anyone decide to attack I didn't stand a chance, they could be on top of me without me ever seeing them.It seemed an age but was only an hour later when the Ratz Lila returned with coffee and a jam sandwich. He apologised for the poor fair. 'Food will be better tomorrow, Yossi is on' he said.

He took two cigarettes out of a carton and offered me one.

'Marlboro lights, American, not that Israeli shit.' he said smiling and holding out one towards me

'I just quit smoking' I replied

'Think it's time you started again' he joked.

I took the cigarette from him. He was right.

I watched him head to the other guard posts, munched my sandwich and returned to my fear. The fog was now much thicker and I still had another fifty two minutes left in this sardine tin. I swivelled the heavy machine gun to a more central position and placed my finger on to the trigger. My finger never moved from the trigger of my gun for the remainder of my shift.

It was only on my tour around the base I realised my fears had maybe been a little exaggerated. The base sat on a small hill between two others, one housing a base of the Lebanese army, the other hill housed the Israeli backed Christian militia. Many Israeli guard posts in Lebanon were converted castles or ready built bases of the Lebanese army or militia. This was assembled from scratch. We were protected by huge concrete walls on four sides with metal gates at the entrance. Maybe I was a little paranoid but the gates appeared incredibly flimsy, especially in contrast to the remainder of the base. I thought of the wolf and the three little pigs. The enemy could probably shell the guard posts until next week without making a dent, but a huff and a puff at the front gate and they were in. Maybe terrorists didn't attack army bases from the gates, maybe that wasn't in the terror rule book.

The roadway from the 'main' road to the entrance was at least a kilometre in length and clearly visible from the guard posts. I thought it strange there was no flag flying above the base. I never asked why. Perhaps they didn't want to draw attention to themselves but then every terrorist in the area knew we were there.

Sometimes our biggest danger seemed to be when the two factions, the Lebanese army and Christian militia, decided to shell each other and we risked being hit by an errant rocket. Neither side were very good with their accuracy and often shells fell a little too close for comfort. We were surrounded by the most stunning scenery. Green rolling hills and olive orchards. The closest town, Hatzbaya, was around five kilometres away to the east. At night you could see the distant flickers of the city lights. They were the only illuminations visible on the landscape. Occasionally we would see a lone shepherd with a few goats or a solitary old battered car drive into the town but most of the time the area was devoid of human life.

Hatzbaya was situated about fifty kilometres to the west of Damascus, Syria, about sixty kilometres south of Sidon and around 120 kilometres south of Beirut. It was actually closer to Syria than the bigger cities of Lebanon. It sat at the foot of Mount Hermon overlooking a deep amphitheatre from which a brook flowed to the Hasbani.

The population was about 5000. Hatzbaya was the capital of the Wadi El Taym, a long fertile valley that ran parallel to the western foot of Mount Hermon. Watered by the Hasbani river, the low hills of Wadi El Taym were covered with rows of silver-green olive trees, its most important source of income. Villagers also produced honey, grapes, figs, prickly pears, pine nuts and other fruit. Mount Hermon, over 2700 metres high, was a unifying presence throughout the Wadi El Taym. This imposing mountain held great religious significance for the Canaanites and Phoenicians, who called it the seat of the All High. The Romans, recognising it as a holy site, built many temples on its slopes. Some identify Hatzbaya with the Old Testament's "Baal – Hermon," while in the New Testament the mountain is the site of the transfiguration of Jesus. Hatzbaya was mainly inhabited by the Druze with some Christians. The locals were not really a threat to the Israeli soldiers posted there but it was a popular thoroughfare for Hezbollah terrorist fighters heading for the Israel-Lebanon border. Hatzbaya was an important historical site, but little of its ancient monuments survived. The oldest standing ruins date to the Crusader period. Hatzbaya kept its traditions alive and its workshops were still producing traditional clothing such as caftans and turbans.

The base was little bigger than the size of a football pitch. The buildings were all metal portacabins. One housed the soldiers, one for the officers, one for the kitchen/dining room, one for the ammunition room and another for the toilets and showers. We made our room as homely as was possible. There was little space with a dozen bunk beds hugging the sides of the metal box. There were no cupboards or closets, we hung our clothes on the side of the beds, on nails or kept them in our kit bags. You soon became immune to the putrid smell of the kitbag which reeked as clean and dirty clothes were mixed together. We had pinned up photographs of loved ones back home or photos from the newspaper of the latest sex symbol half naked.

The walls were filled with graffiti, from song lyrics to even an announcement that 'Kilroy was here'. There were scores of names and dates scribbled over the walls. 'Yossi 10/84, Avi 1/85'. I wondered where Yossi and Avi were now, what impression had this place made on them? Would they be unfortunate to return later in their service? And would they be pleased or depressed to see their name still inscribed on the walls of this tin can. According to the graffiti, Ava was very loose and more than willing to carry out most sexual requests, many of them listed. For those interested, her telephone number was provided. The code was for Ashkelon, too far for me. I pinned up a calendar I had made counting the days down to my discharge. Hardly a professional job but the uneven boxes containing coloured in numbers made it all the more authentic. I would be killed here and years later this authentic artifact of war memorabilia would be sold at auction like some First World War piece of charred, dirty, paper containing a scrawled poem by Wifred Owen. A dartboard hung above the door in a vain effort of giving the room the feel of a social club. I had never seen the darts though. I think the board had been left behind by the soldiers before us and they had either taken the darts with them or lost them. Either way the board was merely for cosmetic purposes. Even had we found the missing darts the board would have been pretty useless as some of the numbers had been shot away. Double twenty was out of the question replaced with a gaping hole.

Extra days food was delivered by convoy each week giving us a food surplus each week. This was security in case a future convoy couldn't get through. A twice weekly convoy brought us food, ammunition, equipment and sometimes telephones to call home. I now realised where the decent food went to in the army. On Base 80, Moshave Sade, Takoa, we had fought for the last chicken leg. Here there was no end to the banquet. Beef and Schnitzel and as much as you could eat, no fight for a second chicken leg. We were never hungry. The kitchen was always unlocked for us to snack between meals. The convoy was also used to ferry soldiers to and from leave. The rotation system, adhered to by everyone without exception or fault, meant that we served seven days on, four days leave. Nobody ever missed their return date. That would mean screwing your buddies as you couldn't leave until they returned. The detachment was split into three units, each guarding a separate base. Each housed around twenty soldiers, a tank and it's three crew.. There was limited contact between the three bases one of which based Ian and Moshe. We would only meet up on the convoy to or from the base or sometimes chat to each other over the tank radio.

Daily at 7am and again just before dusk we would patrol the perimeter of the base and the dirt track to the main road checking for explosive devices or any tampering with the base defences. It was vital the road was safe and clear for the incoming convoys. Twice a week, just before the convoy was due, we would patrol the two kilometre road as far as the United Nations peacekeepers outpost. During daylight it would be virtually impossible to get close to the base to attack or lay roadside explosives but as I found out during the night, with the added fog, it would be easy to get close up. The tank did have equipment to pick up movement around the hills but nothing was infallible. It was my first trip out and I was quite apprehensive. I lifted the radio onto my back and joined the other five soldiers and Yossi, our commander at the gates. While all seemed quiet outside the base, except the odd shepherd or the occasional car along the road heading for Hatzbaya, this was a war zone and all it took was one roadside bomb. As a natural daydreamer it was sometimes difficult to keep my mind on the business in hand. I marvelled at the beautiful countryside. The rolling green hills, the blooming Cyprus trees and the roadside vines. All looked perfectly tended and cared for, none looked the least bit neglected yet you never really saw anybody about. Maybe god was looking after the nature while his people were busy making war. The only sounds I could hear were the crunching of heavy army boots on the gravel track road and the intermittent crackle of the army radio fixed tightly to my back.

I relished my role as radio operator. Under Yuval I was given no responsibility. Had I found myself near a radio I would push it to a fellow soldier. Now the codes just rolled off my tongue. I would answer with confidence. 'Root (roger), Avor (over)'. I'd had no formal training, I wasn't sure there was a course for army radio operators. There probably was, there were courses for most things. The first time I had been handed the radio by Yossi I nervously handed it back explaining I didn't think my Hebrew was good enough. Yossi was insistent and smiling handed me a sheet of codes.

'You'll be fine, just learn the list, tehiye beseder (will be OK)' he said.

I learned the codes. I knew 'Perach', flower, was the code for a dead soldier. I hoped I would never have to use the word. I knew really that in the nightmare scenario of us being attacked or overrun by the enemy, my call for help would be heard from high command whatever language or words I used. I didn't even really feel the weight of the radio. I was a full member of the team, no weight, no burden was too heavy to carry anymore.

As we rounded a bend a white Mercedes car approached slowly. Yossi raised his arm signalling the car to stop while we raised our guns in support. The car came to a halt with the middle aged driver and his elderly passenger getting out of the car with both arms raised. It seemed an age as they got out. My heart raced. The driver clearly knew the procedure as he slowly got out of his car, his hands raised. His passenger followed the same procedure. Both moved slowly to the rear of the car their arms still raised. Yossi raised his gun and lowered it in one quick action signalling the two to lower their arms. The driver handed over his documents without even being asked. No single occupancy vehicles were allowed in the area for fear they were suicide bombers. This rule made it difficult for locals as often they would have to pay people to travel with the driver. We studied as best we could the drivers documents. To be honest my Hebrew was not perfect and my Arabic was non existent. I didn't have a clue what I was looking at. Although he looked confident I wasn't sure Yossi knew either. It could have been the guys television licence for all we knew. I did my best to fake intelligence. Yossi asked them in English where they were going.

'Hatzbaya' replied the driver.

'For what?' asked Yossi

'I take my uncle to the doctor' added the driver.

It was not uncommon for terrorists to use the doctors or the hospital as an excuse to pass through a checkpoint. The hope was that the soldier would be more sympathetic. The two in the car appeared genuine but not genuine enough for me to move my finger away from the gun trigger. The locals, mostly farmers, really just wanted a quiet life as their ancestors had enjoyed for centuries. They didn't care who ruled the country.

They were not interested in politics. They just wanted to farm, to weave clothes and to celebrate weddings and births. They were as angry with the terrorists who had come from the north as they were with the occupying Israelis. Yossi smiled at the driver.

'OK, you carry on' he ordered. The driver thanked the officer as he got back in his car. I thought it sad and remarkable he had thanked the soldier who was invading his country and had inconvienced him by stopping him mid route to an important errand. In reality, although they could never admit it, many locals were delighted with the Israeli occupation. Terrorists would often take over a town or village and wreak havoc on the locals. They would steal food and take what little money or few possessions they had. Often any objectors were shot dead, often in public to make an example. I watched the car move off slowly into the distance confident we had behaved respectfully and treated the locals with dignity.

We arrived at the United Nations base which was guarded by two armed soldiers. They stood firm in their blue berets and neatly pressed olive coloured uniforms. I nodded to one guard but he returned only a stone cold scowl in return. One of my colleagues laughed,

'Don't worry about it, they don't like us much' he said.

The United Nations peacekeepers had been stationed along the Israel-Lebanon border since the 1970s. A small minority had been caught by the Israelis smuggling arms to terrorists across the border into Lebanon. With Israel getting bashed almost daily at the United Nations council, there was no love lost between Israel and the organization. This tension filtered down from the top officials to the soldiers of both sides on the ground. Many U.N. Soldiers would take their leave in the

Israeli coastal towns of Netanya and Herzlyia where there were often fights between U.N. And Israeli soldiers. The majority of the U.N. Soldiers were from Scandinavia and Fiji. Although well paid, they were under great danger often shot at by terrorists with little authorization to return fire. No surprise they were miserable. We rested outside the base lighting a cigarette under the large blue U.N. Flag waving frantically in the heavy wind. I sat on a large rock and finished my cigarette blowing the smoke into the Lebanese countryside. I could see the snow covered Mount Hermon in the distance. I was on the wrong side of the mountain. Yes I felt a lot more comfortable in the army now under Yossi and the others but I felt nostalgic for home.

Chapter 27 If the Kids are United
November 23rd 1985

Under a Blue Moon
(Written by a soldier, preparing for battle)

Full moon rising over Lebanese hills
Soldiers waiting for the kill
Blue moon rising over Maine road
Our Fortune turned?, Berkovic skill !

BBC world service beams across the sea
Motson and Davies carry the news
United collapse under another City onslaught
This is war as the battle ensues

I watch from my lookout,
Our defence solid and ready
We wait on our captain's shout
Our attack potent and deadly

I'll take the right flank, Seany takes the left
We'll hit them hard in the middle, Goater sinks the ball deep
into the net

If I die at Kippax street
Fighting for Colin the king
Forget not the glory of the city
Manchester's only real team
I am here, there, everywhere
Under a blood red Lebanon sky
Yet all I see are blue dreams
I am city 'till I die.


I managed to arrange my guard duty to coincide with the World Service football commentary on the radio. I smuggled in my small transistor radio under my thick winter coat. While we had constant visitors to our guard posts at night, during the day we were left alone. Yossi would probably not have done anything had he caught us with our transistor radios in all probability. At least they kept us awake. The cold had set in and the small heater in the post did not provide the warmest of environments, it did serve well as a toaster. Banana spread on toast was a tasty snack whilst combatting the boredom of staring out at the countryside for hours on end. Sometimes it was difficult to differentiate between the burned bits of toast and the rust from the heater. Hardly restaurant quality or hygiene but it was tasty.

The hope was that City could build on the recent victory over Nottingham Forest. The season wasn't going too well and a victory today over Newcastle United was essential. The radio, and especially the BBC was a lifeline to the world outside. It was strange listening to news about the conflict I was involved in. The trick was to find the middle ground between news reports on the BBC and Israel news. Neither were particularly impartial. I was more interested in the football reports and the entertainment shows on the BBC. I might now be an Israeli, but I still enjoyed much of my British heritage and culture. Now as I looked out towards the Lebanese hills, as I munched on my less than hygienically prepared banana toast, I listened to my radio as Manchester City edged a narrow 1-0 victory over Newcastle United. A goal from Mark Lillis, although a Mancunian, began his career at Huddersfield Town before the recent £130,000 transfer to City. The victory did little to improve our position in the bottom five of the table. And with newspaper reports claiming the club was around £4m in debt, this victory over Newcastle was a little subdued.

On Saturdays the BBC World Service switched from news and entertainment to live soccer commentary. While the news reports always seemed so 'British' with reporters who appeared to be talking with plums in their mouths, Eton and Cambridge educated toffs, the football was the working mans area. To a non English speaker the two languages used were completely different. I loved football on the BBC. While independent television and radio had to big up a poor game for the sake of ratings and its advertising income, if the game was crap the BBC would say it. My favourite commentator was Alan Green. Green had worked in local newspapers until he moved to the BBC in 1975 as a news trainee. I loved his forthright commentary and honest assessments of football games. If the game was poor he would say so. Green had an ongoing feud for over 20 years with Alex Ferguson, the Manchester United manager, 'He either bullies or frightens' said Green. Green had described Manchester City Chinese defender Sun Jihai as wearing shirt 'Number 17, that'll be the Chicken Chow Mein, then' during a live radio broadcast. Green commentated on a match between Everton and Reading at Goodison Park. Film star Sylvestor Stallone was paraded on the pitch and Green joked about whether Stallone's limousine would still have wheels when he returned to it. This prompted an official complaint to the BBC by Liverpool Council upset at his stereotypical views about car crime in the city. I loved Israel but I still missed some things from the home country. I missed my football and the BBC took me back, if only for a couple of hours.

One major lifeline was the phone truck which arrived on the base usually once a week. The large army truck was the strangest thing I had ever seen, even in this strange army. With half a dozen telephones I could now make contact with the outside world. At first I couldn't get a line to England so I made several calls to Israel including Jo and Stella. We chatted for a few minutes amid the chaos behind as soldiers in the queue shouted for us to rush our calls and pass the phone on to them. These were young kids desperate to talk to mom. As important as my calls were, I felt for these kids. I moved away and began chatting to one Israeli called Sidney. Sidney, a young Israeli whose English was probably better than mine, appeared to be the self appointed leader of the group. It was he who first welcomed me into the fold at the beginning. I told Sidney I had tried to call England without success. He explained that he had just called his girlfriend in Sweden, that a special code was needed to get an international connection.

'The army won't tell you that, they wanna keep their phone bill down' he joked.

Suddenly he grabbed me and pulled me towards to phone truck. He pulled me to the front of the queue. 'Let this guy through, he needs to phone Manchester, England' he shouted.

The soldiers moved away like the parting of the Red Sea and I grabbed the receiver. It was the strangest telephone conversation I had ever had. From two thousand miles away on a hill in Lebanon I talked to my parents in Manchester. I told them I was on a base in Israel so as not to worry them but I was sure my father knew the truth. If I was supposed to talk in code I didn't but then I was just so excited to talk to my family. That said I told them little anyway. I knew little. I couldn't tell them troop numbers or operations because I didn't know them and the little I did know I withheld for fear of worrying them. They never argued like they had done when I called from the kibbutz. Perhaps they had decided to put on a united front for my benefit.

It didn't take me long at all to settle in with the Israelis. They found it impossible to understand why I would give up a comfortable middle class, safe, life for all of this. Sidney arrived at the guard post to relieve me following my shift.

'So how old you?' he asked

'Twenty three' I replied

He laughed.'You only look our age, what's that scar on your chin?'

'Oh I fell off a rope swing when I was about twelve' I replied.

He looked out to the Lebanese landscape and sighed. 'So let me get this right, you had a car, a job, money and the most dangerous thing you ever did was fall off a swing? And you came here? Are you fucking mad?'

'Maybe but I feel safe here, feel at home here even with all this 'hara' (shit). I don't know, I can't really explain. I never felt right in England. I could sit in a crowd of people who didn't know I was Jewish, I would hear them talking about Jews, they are all rich, they run the television, the movies, the media, the government they would say and I felt uncomfortable. I hate the religion. I think it's sexist, elitist, racist but there is no escaping I am a Jew. Hitler never spared the Jews that hated the religion, if you were born Jewish you were gassed.'

I looked at Sidney. He looked confused still. 'But why do the army? Just come and live here' he responded.

'It's part of the country and I wouldn't have met guys like you folks' I flattered.

'Don't get it, don't get it at all, the day I finish this shit I'm on a plane to America' he said.

I had just finished my guard duty and usually would have rushed back to my bed but this was important. I wanted to try and understand why hundreds of thousands of Jews all around the world were desperate to move to Israel while so many Israelis were equally as determined to leave the country. I asked Sidney.

'I guess we are tired here. Look at kids my age in England or America,' Sidney continued 'what are they doing? College, working, travelling the world, what the fuck am I doing? Dressed in shit green, eating shit, fighting shit for three years then a month every year. Do you guys look under the seat for a bomb each time you get on a bus? Your politicians argue over raising or lowering tax a penny and other banal stuff, our lot argue over wars and invasions. Life here is so fucking heavy, we are all so tired of it. We just want a normal boring life like everybody else.'

Sidney was passionate and quite upset. I had no answer for him. Perhaps this was just youthful disillusionment though deep down I knew it was more than that.

During our first family visit to Israel all the way back in 1974 we had hired a car and were touring the country. Even my father, a man renowned for his short temper struggled with the Israeli Kamikaze style of driving. One day we stopped and gave two hitchhiking soldiers a ride. Ezra and David were fresh out of a tank division fighting the Yom Kippur war in the Sinai. My parents invited them to join us on a camping trip to the Galilee and surprisingly they joined us. To this day I remember the excitement of posing as a twelve year old boy by the shores of the Lake Kinneret with an Uzi sub machine gun. It's funny how an image now of a young boy posing with a machine gun gives off such a negative image around the world, be it an Israeli or Arab child. We never saw David again but Ezra remained a firm family friend and does so until this day. Like many Israelis he travelled outside Israel after his service and spent several months with us in Manchester. Like many Israelis he could be blunt and stubborn. It was amusing how sometimes my parents struggled with the Israeli mentality. I did too very often. On one occasion my parents brought Ezra a box of chocolates from England. Ezra thanked them for the nice gift and then said 'We are visiting friends tomorrow night, is it OK if we give them these chocolates as a gift?'

My mother was horrified. The British would never do something like that, or if they did, they wouldn't announce it.

On my visits to Israel after Year Course I often spent weekends with him and his parents. They were fluent in several languages, but not English. Ezra was almost word perfect. I remember watching television at weekend understanding little, if anything, that was going on. I looked forward to the American sitcoms and movies. Ezra tried for a long time to dissuade me from enlisting and this angered me. I understood later that following his traumatic service he cared enough about my welfare that he did not want me to go through the same hardship. I was still bitten and infected by the Zionist bug and stopped visiting. He refused to go into details of his war experiences but I can only imagine how harrowing they must have been. During the early days of the Yom Kippur war, Israel, taken by surprise by the Egyptians and Syrians, suffered some terrible losses. There were hundreds of Israelis, Sidney included, who said we were mad, crazy but Ezra was the only one who ever said firmly 'Don't do it.'. To this day I still do not agree with his opinion. You cannot serve as an Israeli citizen without serving in the Israeli army, whatever you do to serve, combat or desk job.

Yossi, our commander had only just seen his twenty first birthday yet here he was making life and death decisions. Of course operation decisions came from a higher authority but when on manoeuvres or attacked ultimately his decisions affect the safety of the entire unit. His soldiers, just eighteen or nineteen years old, also had a huge responsibility. It was a stark reality throughout the country, teenagers, just out of school, walking about the country with automatic machine guns. Imagine that in Britain or America. It didn't bear thinking about.

I never heard Yossi raise his voice. He was softly spoken but loud and clear enough to be understood. It was clear he trusted us and we trusted him to keep us safe. His only inspections were a brief check of our packs before patrols and our outside manoeuvres. He kept himself to himself only seeing him at meal times or on patrol. On the few occasions we encountered any incidents, he was always calm and decisive in his actions. The Israelis were soon like family. Eli was the appointed cook. The kitchen was his empire and nobody was allowed access to anything without going through him. We cooked every day instead of doing guard duty. When he was off duty we ate jam, chocolate spread or banana sandwiches, when on duty his creations were inspired. He would never perform the menial tasks himself seconding others to peel potatoes and wash up. Those tasks were beyond an artist like himself he would claim. With his Arab family background his dishes were often very spicy and the others would often laugh as I almost choked, my mouth on fire from the hot spicy seasoning.

Haim was the father figure amongst the group. He was the one you would find with his arm around a fellow soldier comforting them. For most of the time we were OK. Yes it got cold, we missed our families, our girlfriends. Sometimes we got frightened but on the whole we were a happy bunch. There were mini dramas when a particular soldier just needed a shoulder to cry on and Haim was there for that moment. His talent, even at such a young age, was to defuse a situation or tension before it escalated. Some nicknamed him the diplomat as he always knew the right thing to say. Avi was the clown. I don't think I ever heard him say anything serious but he had a heart of gold. He would give you his last chicken leg if he thought you needed it more than him. When on guard duty he often came to change me ten or fifteen minutes early. We would spend the time chatting and joking together. It seemed like he had gone through a tough childhood. He had spent little time in school and more than an acceptable amount of time in police custody. He was far from stupid but had failed to graduate high school. The army had seemed to have given him the stability he needed. He was a good soldier, not officer material but still a competent soldier. On my low days it was Avi I turned to, or rather he came to me with a joke or a prank. It didn't take long for my smile to return. Sidney was my favourite. One of his grandparents was English and from an early age he had spoken the language at home. While my Hebrew was improving there were still times I couldn't express myself, Sidney was there to help. He was like 'the all American boy' in Israel. Athletic and good looking, blond curly hair and well built, it was obvious he had countless girls waiting for him at home. He seemed to run the group . He organised the rotas for leave. Yossi was fine with this as long as the required number of soldiers were on base. He had helped me with the army telephones. I was the old man here and he treated me with respect.

It was funny that kids so young could have so many dilemmas of their love lives. They were almost all in love, desperately in love, with their high school sweethearts. It was quite endearing. Their youth meant they had no inhibitions and no subject was taboo for discussion. Within a short time I knew their favourite sex position and how far each of their girlfriends would go. Perhaps unsurprisingly Sidney appeared to 'travel' furthest. Many were still virgins and they listened with awe and envy to the sex tales of the experienced. Masturbation was a popular hobby amongst us on the base. With a dozen or so so soldiers in the sleeping quarters the only quiet place was the guard post. Soldiers arriving at the guard post, either changing guards or the Ratz Lila, would announce their arrival giving the 'hobbying' soldier a chance to 'sort himself'. On one of the occasions we discussed this one soldier announced that while he did masturbate he stopped himself from finishing. Shimon was the baby of the group. He looked barely thirteen and like they had mistakenly drafted him during his Barmitzvah Having completed any task he would invariably turn to another soldier for confirmation he had not made a mistake. The truth was he never did make a mistake and was probably our best, most efficient soldier. .

'It's a sin, a waste of a Jewish life' he chirped

'Bullshit, you telling me Moses spent all that time on Mount Sinai, alone, and didn't once masturbate?' joked Sidney

'Hell no, ' butted in Avi 'would you with god watching you, could you do it with someone watching you?'

'Depends who' replied Sidney 'not you' he said looking at Avi.

'Well, I do touch it, stroke it a little and let it get hard but I wont shoot' said Shimon with an endearing innocence.

'So what's the fucking point then?'asked Sidney.

The room broke out in laughter.

Nati was strangely quiet but then he was most of the time. I found his name strange.

'Why Nati?' I had once asked him.

'After Nat King Cole, the singer' he had replied.

I was surprised, most Israelis were given deep and symbolic names. Ariel meant lion of god, Avi, my father, Haim meant life while Yonatan was gods gift.

'Nat King Cole, hardly one of the great biblical Jewish warriors' I said

'Well my parents were fucking to one of his songs and nine months later they couldn't decide on a name so....' We both burst into laughter.

Now Nati sat quietly. He looked uneasy.

'What about you Nati?' chirped Yitzhak 'You jerk off to George Michael? Is it Wham with your cock?'

There was an uneasy nastiness in Yitzhak's tone. We suspected a little that perhaps Nati was gay, without any real justification. He had never said anything, nor done anything overtly gay. He was neither overtly effeminate nor butch. The army did not discriminate against gay soldiers. While in some of the tougher units some soldiers could be somewhat homophobic, most soldiers, like most Israeli citizens, really didn't care.

'What if he was?' I barked at Yitzhak

'You two aren't, you know, a couple are you?'

Of the entire group Yitzhak was the only soldier I didn't like. From the day I had arrived he had been distant and sometimes aggressive towards me. Not physically but often verbally. He was an Israeli with a huge chip on his shoulder.

'You lot come over here from Europe and America with all that money, then get more from our government for doing us a favour by coming over. We eat shit all our lives, you eat shit for a year then fuck off back to London'

'Manchester' I corrected him with more than a hint of sarcasm.

There were many, a small minority, of Israelis like him. They resented us, thought we were just here on an adventure holiday, easy to go back if it got too tough. In hindsight maybe he was right.

'What if he is gay, you think he'd want his 'basar', meat, in your dirty mouth? I continued. I was angry. It was easier letting out the aggression with Yitzhak being the recipient.

'Fuck you,' replied Yitzhak.

'Halas, maspeek, enough' said Sidney in three languages so as sure to make his point.

I got up and headed outside. I needed to calm down. This was my first real outburst in the army. I don't think it was so much the issue of Nats sexuality but a frustration with army life. I was tired and Yitzhak was the perfect target for my anger.

We carried out one of our rare operations outside the base at night. Alerted to possible terrorist activity we moved out around midnight to a kilometre or so away from the base. We lay in a circle on the damp, stony ground our feet touching the soldier next to us. Every few minutes a soldier would tap the soldier next to him to make sure he was awake. At regular intervals during the night we would whisper the number given to us beforehand. Twelve soldiers, twelve numbers. Avi, the class clown, number six, would leave a few seconds before whispering his number. Being number five and with my foot touching his, I knew Avi was still present, Yossi didn't though and must have just been ready to panic when Avi would whisper his number. We lay silent, shivering, our guns covering 360 degrees for five hours without incident. It was cold, uncomfortable and pretty scary. Nothing stirred the entire shift. If there were wild animals in the countryside none ventured close. Of the hundreds of square kilometres in South Lebanon, the chances of a band of terrorists stumbling upon us was pretty remote. In all probability there was a group of a dozen Hezbollah fighters twenty kilometres away lying in a circle, cold and shivering, waiting for an Israeli patrol. It was all so futile. It felt like sometimes we just did some things because we were there, to fill the empty time. Sometimes the threat was real, the danger was real but too often it just felt like we were just kids playing war in their back garden. After five hours lying on the cold ground that night we postponed the game. We would often play basketball or five a side soccer in the base courtyard. We had lost a few balls over the base fence as nobody was prepared to retrieve the lost ball for some strange reason. The nearest neighbours to ask for our ball back were the militia on the neighbouring hill. They weren't the type of people you invited around for afternoon tea or a movie night.

Guard duty was by far the biggest drag in the army. During training the three, four or even five hour guard shifts seemed insane. What were we guarding? Who were we guarding against? We were guarding against the enemy but who exactly was the enemy in a suburban park or in the middle of the Arava desert? The nearest Arab was miles away and there were far more 'attractive' targets. My time in Lebanon, alone at the guard post answered the question finally. We were guarding against ourselves, against our lethargy. We were the last line of defence between the terrorists and the Israeli citizens over the border. One hundred percent concentration was required for two or three hours guard duty. Two hours was a piece of cake when we had done five hours back on training. Lying in a circle half the night in a damp field in total silence was easy when we had done a full night during basic training.

## Chapter 28   I Just Died in Your Arms Tonight
November 29th 1985

What would happen, if we kissed?
What would we do then?
What if we were to lie down together?
If I caressed your gentle skin?

What would happen, if we made love?
What would we feel then?
What if we were to lie down together?
If I tasted your sweet lips?

What would happen, if we had never met?
Where would we be then?
What if we were to lie down together?
If I shared your secrets within?

What would happen, if we shared our dreams?
Where would we go then?
When we lied down together
We touched heaven?

What would happen, if we kissed? What would we do then?

We waited like expectant fathers pacing the delivery ward for our convoy to arrive. Every minute of delay brought frustration and anxiety. It was my turn to go home, if only for four days. Constant shouts to the guard tower facing the road in were met with the same negative reply. Finally, a little after ten in the morning, the convoy arrived. The supplies were unloaded and the returning soldiers greeted those on base. We would not be allowed off base if any had failed to return for whatever reason. Fortunately all had returned and my leave pass was signed by the officer. I spotted Ian on one of the trucks. He was returning to his base on the next hilltop. I got into the same truck throwing my bag packed with dirty clothing inside the truck first. We chatted and laughed as we made the journey to his base to drop off soldiers and supplies before our departure home. It was good to see him.

The short journey to the crossing at Metulla passed without incident. We all joked, excited we would soon be home. A hitchhike to Kiryat Shmona and a short five minute bus ride to Kfar Blum and I was home. It was a nice change from the hours travel home earlier in the service. I arrived at lunch time and entered the Kibbutz dining room still in uniform and gun draped over my shoulder. It was no hero's return. We had alienated many of the members of the kibbutz. Although the girls had finished their active part of the army, they were still required to live on the kibbutz and serve out the period called 'Shalat'. Most did not want to be there and took every opportunity to escape. I had been looking forward to seeing Jo but to my disappointment she was away back in Tel Aviv. Four days home gave plenty of free time in contrast the short weekends we used to get. There was time to organise clean uniforms, purchase luxuries from the kibbutz shop and even do a spot of record shopping in the only department store in Kiryat Shmona. Simon in England had kept me up to date with the music scene giving me a few recommended purchases.

I wrote letters home, to my family, Simon, Dave, work colleagues and of course Ruth, my long distance girlfriend. She was due out during the summer and we made plans to rekindle the relationship. I wrote also to Jo. I felt a little morbid, like I was writing my final letters before my death. I didn't think I was going to die. Maybe I was just being organised. I posted all my letters except the letter to Jo. I left that on my cupboard in my room. I didn't have any real intention of giving it to her, not if I was alive anyway. Maybe I was embarrassed by its contents. We had a strange relationship. I thanked her for her support. Of the whole garin, hers had been the only constant. Todd was gone, and most of the others weren't talking to me. Moshe was there, he was always bloody there but I didn't think he was the best audience for many of my thoughts. Although thoroughly miserable on kibbutz, Jo was happy with Peter, her long term boyfriend. I knew there could never be anything serious or long term between myself and Jo but I wanted her. I was terrified, intimidated even, but horny as hell for her. It was strange. We had grown closer after Todd had left and I had been cut off by Janet and Yaffa. We were deeply miserable and had nobody else close by. I didn't want a life together, even an affair. I just wanted her to screw my brains out. I was terrified and intimidated but drawn to the 'danger'. I dreaded hearing the words 'Is that it?' but still I wanted her. Writing all this in a letter, and letting her find the letter may sound somewhat orchestrated, but it wasn't. I was horrified when, on returning to the base, I remembered leaving the letter in the open in my room. She had a key to my room and was often in while I was away borrowing one thing or another.

The soundtrack of our time in Lebanon was mostly a constant humming of the generator interrupted most afternoons for an hour of mutual shelling between the Moslem and Christian forces on the neighbouring hills. I remembered an episode of the television show MASH called 'Five O' Clock Charlie' where a lone North Korean pilot would fly over the camp every day at exactly five o'clock. He would drop just one bomb that would always fall short of doing any damage. The doctors on the base would sit with home brew cocktails and cheer and jeer the spectacle. Here in Lebanon we watched with the same feelings as the two enemies here launched shells at each other every night. We would hear the missiles scream through the air, see the fire trail light up the sky and watch them fall pathetically short of their targets.

After a short time you didn't even hear the generator. The silence was only broken by the wind. In fact it was so quiet most of the time I can't believe Yossi never heard the transistor radio blaring out from the guard posts. If he did, he never took any action. There was constant shouting but never panic. Most raised voices were complaints when rice was served with chicken for a third day or when yet again the football was booted outside the confines of the base. We would have to wait until the morning patrol to retrieve it.

It was shortly after midnight when I awoke to exploding shells. These were loud and seemed a lot closer than the usual midnight fire show. The portacabin shook as we fell out of beds and into our clothes. We were on duty, fully equipped, within the required three minutes. Our previous training had not been in vain. This was real army, not training, and there were no mock alerts. This was real war. We reinforced the guard posts in case of an attack. The tank on base had spotted movement in the distance and had fired. Before the tank operator could load another shell Yossi was on the radio to the tank.

'What the fuck?' he screamed. The only time I had heard him raise his voice.

'Enemy two kilometres' replied the tank operator.

'So you just decided to fucking shoot, no request from me? Did you check with your commander?' Yossi asked'

'Negative' came the reply.

'So you took your dick out of your hand and thought, hey lets wake up Lebanon, and I bet you fucking missed' barked Yossi.

'Yeh but we were close' answered the tank man.

'Cut the jokes, I ain't in the mood for comedy night' shouted Yossi.

There was no reason for anybody to be walking the hills at this time. The tank radar had pointed out two men and a donkey in the distance. They had opened fire without authorisation and ran the risk of disciplinary action if Yossi reported it, which he didn't in the end. By this time Yossi was dressed and had arrived at the tank. He climbed inside and the argument continued.

'Where are they, show me on the screen' he said.

The tank operator pointed to the black dots on the green screen.

'Heat sources coming towards us' panicked the soldier.

We listened on the radio as the two argued. The tank operator wanted to continue shelling, Yossi wanted them closer. He wanted to see the whites of their eyes. Yossi won the day, kind of, as within a few minutes the figures turned around and ran off into the distance. The incident had lasted almost two hours. We never discovered whether the figures in the night were really terrorists or lost locals. Probably the former as the locals knew not to wander the hills in the middle of the night. Also the story sounds much more dramatic when I say we were attacked by two terrorists rather than we spotted two shepherds and a goat one night in Lebanon.

The night operation that had turned up a blank seemed to have had a strange influence on Yossi. Normally calm and measured he appeared agitated as we patrolled the outside of the base. It was as if he was disappointed he had not seen any action. We spotted two locals dressed in Israeli army uniforms. They were not carrying any weapons or explosives and were just two farmers who had found the uniforms and were trying to keep warm in the winter air. They were handcuffed with cable ties and sat in the wet ground. Yossi was unusually aggressive shouting as we aimed our rifles at the peasant prisoners. Finally satisfied with their answers they were made to take off the uniforms stripping them down to their underwear. Shivering with the cold, and probably fear, the two youths were set free to return to their village. I felt uncomfortable at the incident but understood Yossi had done the right thing. There was no way two civilians could be allowed to roam the countryside in Israeli army uniforms.


I light a candle again this year

Your memory to preserve

An empty space you left us

Every day through my fingers slips grains of earth

I light a candle again this year
Place it by the window
The bright flame helps light our dark world
Can you see it flicker from where you are now

We never heard your cries, never felt the wind
We never knew your fears, never noticed the rain
Maybe had you shouted louder
We wouldn't be lighting a candle again.

I light a candle again this year
With time incrimination and bitterness disappeared
that you left us without a word but still I see Chicago lady's tears.

I spent the morning resting on my top bunk as I was in for a long guard shift later on. It was not difficult switching off from the surroundings. Through my Walkman headphones Van Morrison sang of Cyprus Avenue as I read again of the planets The Little Prince visited on his journey to earth. I declined offers to play star striker in the yard. I was happy in my own company for now. The time passed without really doing much. I never felt bored even though I didn't do much. We did guard sometimes eight hours during the day, another six hours sleep, an hour for each of the three meals, two hours patrol by the time you have checked and double checked your equipment. The day was almost filled. I am mostly reluctant to begin a discussion as I am sure it would end in an argument. I return to my book, the prince has reached the desert and is taming the fox.

My marathon shift began at noon helping prepare lunch for the soldiers. We did not have an army cook, we prepared the food ourselves, sometimes even surprising ourselves with our culinary skills. Following lunch and the clean up I began my role as 'Ratz Lila'. I spent the night making coffee and flirting between the different guard posts spending a little time with each guard. I also woke soldiers when it was their shift. Obviously the guard could not leave his post. I also relieved the guard for toilet breaks. My visits also included the soldiers in the tank. I sat on the top of the tank talking to one of the three soldiers while the other two slept.

'Where you from?' asked the gunner

'Manchester' I replied

'Not much difference between Manchester and Lebanon eh?' joked the gunner.

He went on to tell me one of the soldiers on the other base had an English girlfriend. He radioed his colleague and for the next hour we chatted intimately on the promiscuity of English women over the army radio. Heaven knows what any Arab radio hackers must have thought.

One of the greatest fears whilst covering guard duty was that your relief guard would not turn up. You basically had nowhere to go, there was nothing you could do. If he didn't show you couldn't really leave your post to go get him. In combat you risked the safety of your comrades by leaving your post empty. On a safe base you risked punishment from your officer that would, without exception, include cancellation of home leave. If you did leave your post to wake your replacement, if you were lucky he had simply overslept. If he refused to get up, you were screwed. There was no choice but to do another shift and confront the offender the following morning. This was rare but did happen. There had to be, and was mostly, mutual respect between soldiers. We were all tired, none of us wanted to sit in the dark alone for two hours in the middle of the night, but if one refused, all would refuse and anarchy would ensue. On the one occasion I was stiffed by my replacement, early in my service, I did get my revenge. The guard duty rota was worked out by ourselves not the sergeant or officers. So angry by the soldiers actions at refusing to get out of bed, the soldier organising the rota placed him after myself the following night. Payback as now I refused to get up and replace him leaving him to cover my shift.. He never did it again. Ratz Lila avoided this problem as there was a designated soldier to drag the replacements out of their cosy sleeping bags.

Chapter 29 New Years Day

December 25th 1985

Christmas day, Nineteen eighty five

The shooting ceases , To celebrate a life.

Lebanese cedars replace firs, Peaks display their proud snow

Joy that is a silent night, Can't we grow peace from this embryo?

Christian orphans await their father on one hill, Moslem
orphans wait on theirs

Jewish soldiers stand down in the middle, Maybe after tonight
man will finally care.

Christmas day, Nineteen eighty five

Could this be the first, Of many silent nights?


It had been a year now since I sat dejected on the lawn at the
army medics course. Again I listened to The Queens speech on
my radio. I was hardly the greatest royalist, in fact, if anything
I was more of a republican but here all that distance from
England and my family seemed to vanish. Being Jewish,
Christmas was not celebrated but due to the family business it
was an important time. We were always very busy up to
Christmas Day and we would celebrate the rest, and profits, if
not the religious day itself. I missed the Christmas television
shows and even the German version of silent night. As the
BBC World Service played carols of peace from Westminster
Abbey the tracer bullets in Lebanon lit up the night sky. I
watched as the Moslems offered the Christians on the next hill
the gift of gunfire and the Christians duly reciprocated. The
year came to end in Lebanon, twenty one days since I had been
off the base and over six weeks since I had spoken to my
family back in England. A quick review of the year.................

January saw the end of basic training and we were still hurting
from Stuart's suicide the previous month. February and March
were really tough as Yuval, the boy wonder, piled on the
pressure. It was a relief escaping to ulpan in Haifa. May was
spent in England. It was obviously good to see family and

friends but I think maybe I expected too much. June I was patrolling the border back with the unit before being sent off with six other soldiers to build and prepare our next base at Takoa near Jerusalem. Three weeks away from the main unit and although it was hard work but actually good fun. We were our own bosses and managed a couple of free weekends. I remember one Friday deciding at the last minute to leave for the weekend. I threw my bag over my shoulder and ran down the hill towards the dirt track road. Passing civilian cars and buses were a non entity, passing army cars were rare. I spotted a white Renault with army plates just as I hit the bottom of the hill. The driver stopped and the passenger, clearly a general judging by the amount of pips on his shoulders, looked at me, a half dressed, messy soldier wheezing in front of him. It was time for the lonely soldier story. My family were all in England and I had just got word my father was very sick, I had to get home to call him up. The story had more holes than Swiss cheese but he bought it. I was spared a court martial and given a lift to Jerusalem.

In July we were supposed to move on to 'Gdud 50' paratroopers course with the rest of the unit but our garin, under pressure from High Command, opted to do Batash again although quite a few lowered their profiles and moved to join the girls. Just myself, Ian and Moshe were left. We joined an Israeli unit. From July to mid October we were back on the training fields with our new Israeli friends and a decent officer. I was finally a soldier. October I returned to England mainly for my sister's wedding. Ruth visited from America spending a week in Manchester, the highlight being a blow job in the car in Altrincham town centre. November I returned to join my troops in Lebanon.

It was while waiting at the Golan base for my lift to the Lebanon that I saw Jeremy waiting for a lift to a different base. I had missed him. We hugged and chatted until our rides arrived. On his trip home to the states he had been involved in a motorcycle accident spending three months in hospital. As the year went on and as the garin became more fragmented I found myself visiting the kibbutz less often opting to visit various other friends. Over the year I drifted away from quite a few people and much closer to others. Jo was a true friend always there for my lows, and there had been quite a few. I wait for the year to turn. 1986 will see me end my army, move to kibbutz. I can see the roller coaster ride continue.

Chapter 30 It's a Long Road

January 9th 1986

Our replacement troops entered the base with more of a whimper than a bang. One more guard duty shift and then this crazy odyssey would be over. There seemed nobody about, not in the village off in the distance, not in the hills around us. I put the bread on the heater and peeled a couple of bananas. This was my last Lebanon toasted snack. Delicious. We were in a war zone where Christians and Moslems were killing each other, where Hezbollah terrorists were trying to slip into Israel and kill Jews. Religion was fucked. Yet amazingly we had seen little trouble, little damage. It all seemed so perverse.

I took out my diary opening it at the middle pages giving me two clean sheets of paper. I drew myself a calendar for my last thirty days of real army service. After that it would be six months on kibbutz with the occasional training exercise but at least no more running up mountains or manning road blocks.

11am. Finally, our orders confirmed, we jumped aboard the armoured carriers before speeding out of the base. We were met at the bottom of the dirt road by soldiers from the other bases. I spotted Ian and Moshe and waved like some child excited at a toy shopping trip. The Israeli flag flew high above our vehicle. The convoy moved with purpose through the hills and local villages. It wasn't long before had reached Metulla. We sounded our horns and cheered as we crossed back onto Israeli soil. We headed for our new base on the wet, muddy Golan Heights. This was our new home, but only for the next thirty days. Myself, Ian and Moshe reunited hugged each other. We were the last three guys of Garin Nesher.

The Golan Heights borders Israel, Lebanon, and Jordan. According to Israel, it captured 1,150 square kilometres. According to Syria the Golan Heights measures 1,860 square kilometres of which 1,500 are occupied by Israel. According to the CIA, Israel holds 1,300 square kilometres. In the Middle East where disagreement is king, nobody can even agree on the size of the area held by Israel. The area is hilly and elevated, overlooking the Jordan Rift Valley which contains the Sea of Galilee and the Jordan River, and is itself dominated by the 9,000 ft tall Mount Hermon. Internationally recognised as Syrian territory, the Golan Heights had been occupied and administered by Israel since 1967. It was captured during the 1967 Six-Day War, establishing the Purple Line. On 19 June 1967, the Israeli cabinet voted to return the Golan to Syria in exchange for a peace agreement, although this was rejected after the Khartoum Resolution of September 1, 1967. In the aftermath of the 1973 Yom Kippur War, in which Syria tried but failed to recapture the Golan, Israel agreed to return about 5% of the territory to Syrian civilian control. This part was incorporated into a demilitarised zone that runs along the

cease-fire line and extends eastward. This strip is under the military control of United Nations peacekeepers.
Approximately 10% of Syrian Golan Druze accepted Israeli citizenship. There are around forty Israeli settlements on the Golan.

This was a country with so many contrasts, people and land. Almost all of our army service had been spent in the heat of the desert in the south. Now we found ourselves in the rocky, mountainous, cold, barren Golan. Settlements were scattered miles apart. The Israelis were internationally applauded for managing to turn the desert into farms, the Golan deserved the same amount of credit. The Golan gave us an Israeli Winter. It had been a while since I had experienced such a wet downpour. The rain battered the roof of the army bus and I drifted to thoughts of the Manchester rain I had left behind. The bus rocked as we sped through water filled pot holes on the road. Water splashed up against the windows. Most of the Golan appeared cordoned off minefields. Yellow, rusted signs shouted 'Danger' in Hebrew, Arabic and English. The signs also displayed a rather haunting image of a skull and crossbones perhaps for the tourist backpackers unfamiliar with the three languages.

We arrived at the base, a collection of around a dozen tents in a circle around a flapping Israeli flag that had clearly seen better days. My bet was the flag had been planted by victorious troops in 1967 and had borne the elements of hot summer sun and cold blistering winters ever since. Aside from our digs there was nothing for miles other than rocks and mud. There was as much mud inside the tent as there was outside. I put my kitbag on the camp-bed to avoid the mud. It would serve as a useful, if lumpy, pillow. The mud was everywhere, including I'm certain, the coffee. Actually I think the coffee was the mud, it certainly tasted like it was. Had I not been just a few weeks from the conclusion of my service I would have sunk into a huge depression. The young Israelis, who still had more than half of their service yet to complete were visibly shocked and depressed at the sight of the base. I was cold, even with a T-shirt, long johns, army fatigue shirt, sweater, thick army coat and furry woolen hat but I was fine, happy even. Yes it was cold and wet but no worse than I had experienced for twenty odd years in England. I was a month away from army service completition and the base was less than an hour from the kibbutz, a big improvement from the five, six, seven hours bus ride from previous bases in the south. It was good to be reunited with Ian and Moshe. We would be together now until the end.

We were all given leave for the weekend. The three from Garin Nesher had just twenty days left while the young Israelis still had another year of service. I returned to Kfar Blum with Moshe where we were met with a whole lot of changes. Janet and Yaffa had finally moved to another kibbutz. Susan had left Nahal altogether. Jeff was still serving in the commando unit. Myself, Moshe, Peter, Yael, Laura and Jo were all that remained of Garin Nesher to Kfar Blum. It was the first time I had seen Jo since I had left her 'my death letter'. I felt a little nervous. She told me she had read it but said nothing more.

Suddenly I felt a hard slap on my back. I turned around to see Jeremy standing proud in front of me. We hugged. I had missed him. Even though he was not in our garin, he had visited our kibbutz often. He was thought of as a member of Garin Nesher. We all sat together exchanging war stories from Lebanon and the kibbutz. Jeremy filled us in on the other members of his garin. The beers flowed and we laughed for hours. The kibbutz, not having learned the lessons of our garin, decided to take on a second. From this group I got myself a new kibbutz room-mate, Stephen. We only ever met once as our leave time fell at different weekends. When my time for 'shalat' came I would get my own room. As with every other weekend most of my time was spent preparing for the return to base. The difference this time was this would be my last leave before the end of the army.

Had this been the start of the army I would have been deeply depressed on the Golan. I could see Kfar Blum in the distance. I was homesick. The rain never seemed to stop and the mud grew deeper by the day. There was no training and boredom soon set in. I even volunteered for kitchen duty to help pass the time. Our job of cleaning the armoured personnel cars took just two days even on a go slow. My calendar said fourteen days to go. I was wrong. Manchester City had improved their form a little with victories over Nottingham Forest, Newcastle, Coventry City, Liverpool and Southampton. Division One safety was looking probable.


January 23rd 1986 It's over

I woke around 7am, lit a cigarette and grabbed my wash bag from under my bed. I slipped my boots onto my bare feet and headed for the showers. The cold shower removed little, if any, of the splattered mud off my body. I returned to my bed and opened a magazine. This army life was really tough without training or guard duty. Without warning Yossi entered our tent. It was highly unusual for an officer to enter the soldiers tents, they would usually send their sergeants. Pointing at myself, Ian and Moshe, and with a huge smile he told us we had one hour to report outside his tent with all our field equipment returned and cleaned. He would then give us our exit passes. We were going home. As we had no training or guard duties and were really just sitting around Yossi had arranged an early exit for us. Once again he had done the decent thing. Just like the taxi at the start of the army, this army was full of surprises. Our colleagues in the unit helped rally around. They were genuinely happy for us even though they still had another year to serve. The few pieces of equipment we were missing were replaced by other soldiers in the unit, they helped us clean our guns and other equipment. I took a bottle of cheap bubbly from my kitbag and to the cheers of all around, shook the bottle before popping the cork. I took a swig before passing the bottle around my comrades. Within the hour we were stood by the roadside, signed passes in our pockets, waiting for a hitchhike back to civilization. There were no bus services here, we just had to wait for an army vehicle to pass and flag it down for a lift. I was prepared to walk if needed. I was just glad to be out. It was not long before an army truck on its way south pulled up by the roadside. We climbed in the back barely sitting down before the truck sped off, direction Kiryat Shmona.

Chapter 31 Will You?
January 24th 1986


I went back to the place
Of those hedonistic days
Where one nights love was forever
Promiscuity our only endeavour


Behind locked doors, blinds shut tight
We held onto our hats for the ride
And under flaking emulsion
We conquered a mountain called passion


No conflict of emotions, no war of words
No false promises lest the joy be disturbed
Our love under flaking emulsion
This seedy room our heaven


I shall stay here a little while
Breathe in the air and close my eyes tight
Now I can see your corn coloured hair
Now I can say thank you and good-bye.

My meeting with the kibbutz secretary was most uncomfortable. Not only did I have to deal with a barrage of criticism over the previous nights party, which kept much of the kibbutz members awake much of the night, but also I was nursing the mother of all hangovers. We were supposed to be discussing my next six months on kibbutz, where I would live and work. Instead I was warned that the kibbutz was close to throwing the remaining garin members off the kibbutz and my orgy the night before did not help our cause. I spent the long meeting apologising and fighting back the puke. I was now moving into a new stage. 'Shalat'. Six months living and working on Kibbutz Kfar Blum. Technically I was still a soldier and would not be fully released from the army until July or August but this would be a whole lot easier than the real army. Well it would be physically, I wasn't so sure mentally but for now I was set for a considerably easier ride.

The time on kibbutz gave me the opportunity to delve back into my music collection. For six months after leaving Grammar School with less than impressive examination results, I attended the Abraham Moss College to resit some subjects. The college library housed thousands of music albums for rental of a nominal fee. By the end of my brief study period I had copied hundreds of tapes. With these bootleg tapes and the tapes and vinyl I had purchased I probably had over three thousand albums. My taste bordered on schizophrenia with a collection of music from Dvorak to The Stones, The Stranglers to Barry Manilow. At the end of the college time I had marginally improved my qualifications but had impressively improved my music collection.

March 10th 1986  Frustrated Mans Dream


My heart empty for so long now filled with longing
and desires
Your doubts painful but understandable
The agonising wait for you to walk my way.


Every night I caress your soft skin, kiss your sweet mouth
and dive
into the deep blue of your diamond eyes.
Every night I pray you make your first visit to my sacred tomb.
Cast off those clothes of doubt
and fill your heart as I have filled mine.
Together we will share a passion tasted by few.
Follow me into surrender, into passion, into love.

Tattoo

Do you remember that humid night
remember the nerves, the heat, the fright
Crickets calling our names from the dark
words failed me, my throat so dry and tight

A thin sheet separated us from lost innocence
worn away your intrepid resistance
You captured my every burning, every desire
your touch released every bit of me, all of the fire

I never knew what hit me when you came
The feeling of belonging as you called out my name
I could only surrender to your deep blue eyes
I'd be fulfilled now if my existence expired

That moment is tattooed on my beating heart
Where two cigarettes lit up the dark
Hush my love no need to speak
Everything was just so complete.

# April 15th 1986 Zahal : A Love Story

When the sun sets, over a thousand deserts
and my heart
beats through your deep blue eyes
and I will always remember
your gentle touch
that brought us so close
I remember,
the day I found my love.
When the wind blows, and you hold me
like no other ever did,
and for that moment it's real
and I will always remember,
the taste of your lips
that brought us this love,
and I will remember
your laughter and your joy.
And when the sun rises over the mountains
and when the day is hard and the pain sets in
I remember the love that brought us close
I remember the lips I tasted love
I remember the touch that brought us close
I remember our love we had it all.

April 29th 1986 Hold Within Your Heart

Hold within your heart a dream
And let it guide you well.
Play with it when you're feeling low,
Promise yourself you'll never tell.
Your dream will be there just for you,

Be yours, and only yours alone,
Inside your heart, hidden out of view,
Reaping seeds you have sown.
The dream I wish for you is bright,
Healing and lightening your days
Discover all that you can and might
As you love in your unique ways.
Your thought for others.


Jo finally mentioned my letter. She teased me without making me feel uncomfortable. To the casual observer my suggestion, my desire to sleep with her appeared ridiculous. She was beautiful, sexy and assured, I was puny and a nervous wreck. She was, as some may say, out of my league. At the risk of sounding overly profound, love is a simple, lazy word. I remember being chastised at school for using the word 'nice'. It is a lazy word as the author cannot be bothered to seek out better, more descriptive adjectives. So too with 'love'. You love your family, your girlfriend, your pet, your car, a particular movie, ice cream. All different loves, all different emotions. I can't speak for Jo or anybody else affected by our affair. I can only relate my feelings, my story.

Our affair was not planned. It was not some conspiracy to wrestle her away from her boyfriend and for us to skip away into the sunset. I was a wreck, barely eating and surviving on coffee and cigarettes. Everything I had truly believed in, Israel, the army, the kibbutz, the garin family, had, at that time anyway, turned to dust. I wasn't so naïve as to have thought it would all be perfect but I certainly thought it would've been better than it was. I was like a child in pain that needed hugging, comforting, loving. Where nothing around me seemed true anymore I needed truth and honesty. Jo gave me that. I knew it wasn't for ever. I didn't want forever. I didn't need forever but I needed at that moment. I have a love for Jo totally unique. Just as The Little Prince tamed the fox Jo tamed me and once tamed I saw what was important in love and friendship. Sadly for her, as you become responsible forever for what you have tamed, she has spent the rest of her days worrying about my welfare. But she is my rose, unique and unlike any other rose in the world, and I will protect her whenever she may need protecting. Love is not just simply gazing into each others eyes but in gazing outward together in the same direction. True love and friendship is forever, and the more you give, the more you keep. The most important people in your life are the friends who love you when you aren't very lovable, someone who walks in when everybody else walks out. My world was often an awful, frightening place without Jo.

There are few people I respect as I do Peter. On discovering the affair he acted with a dignity I admire to this day. Jo left the kibbutz for a couple of weeks. Peter who had often visited Jo on kibbutz took a little while to visit again. When he did we watched the football together in my room. We laughed together watching Fawlty Towers, we sang together at a Waterboys concert. And when I passed out at the concert he took me to his home and fed me. Years later both our families took holidays together. We are probably the only two people on the planet with the capacity to complain at Disneyland. In my experience, Peter is the most decent person I have ever known, Jo the most caring person I have ever known. One of my great achievements in life is to have earned their love and their friendship.

Chapter 32 That's Entertainment

May 3rd 1986

For Manchester City, after their victory over Queens Park Rangers at the start of February, there was not another win. Four draws, including a 2-2 draw with United at Old Trafford, and a horrific nine losses saw us finish the season in fifteenth place. Just four points above the relegation zone was nothing really to chant about although at least we had avoided relegation in our first year back in the top flight. A new competition, created primarily as a result of the ban of English clubs in Europe, did see City reach the final of the Full Members Cup. City lost an exciting final 5-4 to Chelsea. City youth also beat United youth 3-1 in the FA Youth Final. Seven of the City youth side would later play in the first team. If the present was a little precarious, at least the future looked optimistic. Lillis and Davies finished the season as joint top scorers with fifteen goals each, more than the rest of the squad combined. Manager Billy McNeil left the club to manage Aston Villa. Captain Paul Power, after over 350 appearances for City, left to join Everton. Jimmy Frizzell joined City as new manager.

I spent much of my free time in the Hamashbir department store in Kiryat Shmona buying up music. On my rare visits to

Tel Aviv copy tapes were a bargain at the stalls around the bus station. I was always ready to listen to something new and some of my good friends were always there to promote their favourite tunes. Simon in England kept me in the know what was going on back there. The music charts had changed drastically since I had left England. The Jam had become The Style Council, The Stranglers had gone pop, and crap, and The Clash had just gone. Bowie had reinvented himself from immense Ziggy Stardust to a half decent Modern Love. I was highly impressed that kibbutz volunteer Nigel knew every lyric to every Bowie song. I struggled with the new music now, perhaps I was now like all oldies looking down on modern music. I was less than impressed the pop junk turned out by the likes of Duran Duran, Wham, The Pet Shop Boys and the rest. There was, however, some pretty awesome stuff coming through. Jo bought me REM's first album, The One I love becoming a firm favourite.

I travelled to Tel Aviv to meet up with Jo and Peter at the Liquid Club to attend a Waterboys concert that lasted three and a half hours. Actually it lasted longer but due to the heat of the small concert venue and my lack of a decent meal in several weeks, I passed out before the end of the concert. Israel was not really a popular destination for foreign bands to tour. Besides the security issues many promoters just do not believe the fan base is large enough to sustain a decent profit for the band or promoter. That said, when a band does tour the coverage is immense. Israeli radio stations will play the artists music for weeks beforehand. Their arrival at the airport is similar to a royal visit. An artist with a moderate ego cannot help but be amazed by the reception. The Waterboys were on a six night tour, longer than the usual one or two nights. The band began with a slow version of Don't Bang The Drum followed by Medicine Bow, Be My Enemy before moving on to two of my favourites Fisherman's Blues and The Thrill Is Gone / And The Healing Has Begun. I wasn't sure who I was more mesmorised by, Mike Scott on vocals or Steve Wickham on fiddle. His fingers danced so quickly along that fiddle he would often break a string yet appear to replace the broken string whilst still playing. It was magic as the band continued through Spirit, The Pan Within, This Is The Sea, A Girl Called Johnny and finally before I hit the deck, A Pagan Place.

Jeremy introduced me to the strange yet brilliant Frank Zappa. The album, Sheik Yerboutti, featured Zappa's satirical and otherwise humorous or offensive material. 'Bobby Brown' is well-known worldwide, except for the USA, where it was banned due to its sexually explicit lyrics. 'I Have Been in You' pokes fun at Peter Frampton's 1977 hit 'I'm in You' while maintaining a sexually driven structure. 'Dancin' Fool', a Grammy nominee, became a popular disco hit despite its obvious parodical reflection of disco music. 'Jewish Princess', a humorous look at Jewish stereotyping, attracted attention from the Anti-Defamation League, to which Zappa denied an apology, arguing: 'Unlike the unicorn, such creatures do exist—and deserve to be 'commemorated' with their own special opus'. During my year in Israel my new American friends introduced me to the past American folk scene ignored in England.I had never heard of Harry Chapin, Jim Croce, Dan Fogelberg and James Taylor.

Israel's first attitude towards rock music was extremely negative. The first Israeli rock bands began performing in the mid-1960s in nightclubs and discos, first in Ramla and later on Hamasger Street in Tel Aviv. These bands mainly performed cover versions of popular rock songs by bands like The Beatles and The Shadows. Rock culture, in the social and political sense, was nowhere in sight. Near the end of the decade rock and roll gained legitimacy. Western musicians arrived in Israel, and influences of the pop revolution permeated local culture. Some of the local bands added English musicians to their ensemble, creating several new bands that were based on the original rhythm bands. Between the 1960s and the 1970s, successful Israeli musicians showed interest in rock music, and many of them recorded songs in the rock style by themselves or with bands. The artist who took the most significant step towards the adoption of rock as a dominant force in Israeli music was the popular singer Arik Einstein.. Einstein's albums from those years are considered to be groundbreaking in the way in which they combined rock melodies with Hebrew texts. They demonstrated fresh musical perception and created more personal mainstream songs rather than those of the military bands that dominated the previous decade.

In the early 1970s, Israel had a burgeoning progressive rock scene. During the 1980s a few rock bands became popular. Notable rock bands of the decade were The Click, Benzin, Tislam, and Mashina which became the most successful Israeli rock band of the decade. Although I hadn't grown up with Israeli music as I had done with so many British artists, some like Arik Einstein, David Broza, Si Himan and Shalom Hanoch, all offered songs that became the soundtrack to my life.

During my year in Israel in 1980 Arik Einstein released 'San Francisco Al ha-mayim', San Francisco on the Water, from the album Hamush Bemishkafaim – Armed With Glasses. Although he sang about San Francisco, about how beautiful the place was yet he missed Israel, his home, 'Suddenly I want to go back home, Return to the swamp, To sit in Kasit with Moshe and Chatske. Give me Mount Tibor, Give me the Kinneret. I love and keep falling in love with my little Israel

Warm and Charming' I replaced San Francisco for Manchester. The song expressed my emotions and feelings perfectly. The song became my Aliya song. At the conclusion of Ulpan on Kibbutz Tzuba we had put on a show for the Kibbutz. We included a sketch featuring the song by Yonatan Gefen, 'Ha Yalda Ha'yafe be Gan', 'The prettiest girl in the kindergarten' where of course I dressed up as that girl.

Shlomo Artzi's albums 'Layla Lo Shaket' 'Restless Night', 1986, and 'Hom Yuli August' 'July August Heat', 1988 were inspirational to me and are milestones of Israeli 1980s songwriting. The albums sold in excess of a hundred thousand copies, an unprecedented achievement in the Israeli music industry. On Hom Yuli Artzi sang 'What I remember from this I write down, catch a Haifa taxi, jump to the discotheque, prostitutes on the fence, in me just a ghost burns, I go dancing with dead soldiers in my heart, Write it down, write it down; I write, I write...' I had grown as an Israeli. I had gone from an Englishman pining for the promised land to the prettiest girl in the kindergarten finally to the Israeli soldier. I had served in the army and understood and felt at one with the lyrics. In Israel everybody was both a soldier and a civilian, not one or the other like in most other countries. To survive the country you had to leap from the army base to the nightclub without fear or hesitation less you were doomed.

There was the fun and irreverence of Israeli rock. In 1985 'Waiting For Messiah' 'Mekhakim Le Mashiakh' by Shalom Hanoch sang 'The public is stupid and so the public will pay, what comes with ease with the same ease will go, the little citizen is forced to pay in big, and what interests me is Yardena more than all else, goes off to reserve duty and counts the money that isn't there, And Messiah's not coming - and he's also not calling'. There was the song that told the tale of the

212

man who spent an evening at a bar consuming rather a lot of alcohol before taking a beautiful lady home at the end of the night, only to discover in the morning 'ze lo geveret, ze adom' 'it's not a lady, it's a man'. Mashina told the tale of an Israeli football club so good they could beat Manchester City. In truth, right now, that was no real achievement.

In the late 1980s as I was passing through Israeli army and society Israeli pop/rock became more forceful. 'Ani ve ata neshane et haolam' you and I will change the world and David Broza telling us 'yihie tov' 'it will be ok' as he watched Sadat of Egypt arrive in Tel Aviv were old hat. As with America some years before Dylan was no longer 'Blowing in the Wind', instead Springsteen was 'Born in the USA'. In Israel artists like Si Himan dropped the softly softly approach and angered at least half the population telling us that you were not necessarily a hero soldier for bombing Beirut or patrolling Nablus. Her albums of 1987 and 1988 were of a lady well and truly pissed off. 'Shooting and Crying' is a song about the intifada. It lets the audience, many just shy of army call up, share in the frustration and despair of the past two years. "They shoot and they cry. They burn and they laugh,' she sings, 'When did we learn to bury people alive? When did we forget we too had children killed?' She has sang about domestic violence, poverty and homosexuality.

'The Road From Beit Alpha' she notices that the road passes through the Arab village of Wadi Ara and is 'paved with madness' Mount Gilboa looks on in silence as Kibbutz Beit Alpha is besieged by hypocrisy; the Arab field hands and the Arab prisoners in jail nearby put the lie to the kibbutz ideals of equality. 'The Road From Beit Alpha" also reunites her with her father who wrote so many tunes about the fields and the flowers, the same fields and flowers. Said Himan, `He saw in the landscape the country that he hoped I would grow up in, and I see in it the country that today is not a dream, not of my parents, not of the children of my parents, and not of the children I hope to have. It's exactly the same flowers and fields, but a different time. I write about the same thing he wrote about, but 20 years later. Twenty years of conquest later. But during those 20 years, I didn't realise what a hurricane we are in. `All I'm thinking about is that we're missing a paradise here. I'm very naive; I used to think that it's possible. I'm not so sure anymore.' With Si Himan, Israeli rock had grown up.

My soundtrack of life included Five Years, Bowie the pains of Grammar School. Everybody's gotta learn sometimes, Korgis, teen first love of Lucy in Glasgow. Angie, The Rolling Stones, sang incredibly out of tune by myself and Simon as we wandered to Broughton Park for a football kick about. The entire Astrel Weeks album, Van Morrison, teenage days spent trying to understand the world, and giving up.Mr. Clean, The Jam, teenage days spent hating the world. No more heroes, The Stranglers, God Save the Queen, Sex Pistols and London Calling, The Clash continued the theme. At Seventeen, Janis Ian, things at twenty one I wish I'd known at seventeen. Bookends, Simon and Garfunkel, Never be the same, Christopher Cross, Time in a bottle, Jim Croce, Good-bye Stranger, Supertramp, my friendships of Year Course in Israel 1980/1.To the morning, Dan Fogelberg, the song playing as I lost my virginity. The Letter, Dean Friedman, the crazy odyssey of Aliya. I guess that's why they call it the blues, Elton John, the soldier leaving his love, Ruth, for war. Tupelo Honey, Van Morrison, Ruth gone, Shannon my new sweetness. Ohio, Neil Young, expressed the politician in me. Will You, Hazel O'Connor, the hesitant lover in me. Hotel California, The Eagles, seemed to capture my life in Israel, with the lyrics 'You can check out anytime but you can never leave'. I just died in your arms, Cutting Crew, the love of one already taken.


Chapter 33 Lord is it Mine

June 25<sup>th</sup> 1986

**Life on the kibbutz had been intense over the weeks.** Affairs aside, Shannon had replaced Ruth as the love of my life. She too was an ex American class pupil returning for a visit when we met. We rapidly became inseparable. While Ruth had been quite reserved, Shannon was a wild child. Ruth had never approved of me smoking hashish while Shannon actively encouraged me. I still wasn't eating properly and was stoned most nights. We talked, we talked a lot and when we weren't talking we were having sex. One day the subject of my adoption came up.

'So how old were you when you were adopted?' Shannon asked

'About a week old I think' I replied

'So what about your real parents?' she pushed

'Dunno, I was just told when I was about twelve that I was adopted, given the you are special story and that's it. I don't know anything about them but these are my real parents, the ones that picked me up when I fell. They are the ones shitting themselves when I am in the army.' I added.

'So really you may not be Jewish, huh, you could have done all this shit for nothing' said Shannon.

It got me thinking. What if really I wasn't Jewish. Well I was Jewish, I had the penis to prove it but what if I wasn't born Jewish. Did it really matter? Even if I wasn't I loved this country. There were plenty of non Jews in Israel. Many had just arrived on a visit and had fallen in love with the country and stayed. I had been through the Jewish rituals of circumcision and Bar Mitzvah. I ate chicken soup when ill. It made me think though. I had never seen my birth certificate, let alone the army. I filled in my applications for immigration in England before I came out. On arrival in Israel I glided through immigration to kibbutz to Bakum without being asked to produce my birth certificate. Really how did they know who I was? I didn't even really know who I was.

My highs were incredibly high but the lows were crippling. Jo made me an amazing present. She painted a picture of The Little Prince on a white T-shirt for me. It was incredible. I remember some years ago Simon buying me a huge painting of James Dean walking down the boulevard of broken dreams in the rain. He had spent his first ever paycheck on me and I was hugely touched. This gift from Jo gave me the same feeling.

Moshe was the butt of our pranks. Sadly it was impossible not to pick on him. We were desperate to top our previous prank of hiding his bike, on his own roof. He had spent two days looking around the kibbutz before we finally took pity on him and stood outside his door pointing skywards. I often teamed up with volunteer Nigel. One night, completely out of it, we made a tape of songs he had written about some members of the kibbutz. With our makeshift instruments including a wrist watch alarm, tin pans and spoons we libelled several of the kibbutz members not least a certain Mrs L asserting her hat had gone on holiday. To our dismay, the tape found its way to the kibbutz members who were far from impressed. Again we were dragged into the office and admonished like naughty schoolboys. This did nothing to improve our standing on the kibbutz. Myself, Peter and Nigel retrieved a dead chicken from the chicken house and late in the evening tied it to some

216

fishing wire before sneaking into Moshe's room and placing it behind the blinds above his bed. We waited for him to go to bed before cutting the wire from outside his window. By this time quite an crowd had gathered. It was not easy keeping everybody quiet. Seconds after his light had been switched off, the quiet of the kibbutz was shattered by a scream of 'You bastard Johnny'. How did he know?

My time on kibbutz was one of my loneliest I had ever experienced. My dreams had been shattered. I had not been the great warrior I dreamed of before the army. The first year under Yuval had been something of an embarrassment although I had somewhat redeemed myself afterwards, still not a Navy Seal though. I arrived back to Kfar Blum amid chaos and anarchy. My garin family had fractured and separated. Most had departed and amongst those who remained one half refused to talk to the other half. At least Jo remained and even though her depression seemed greater than mine, without her help I doubt I would have made it through the period. I lived on coffee and cigarettes and lost weight dramatically. There were days she would force-feed me. Members of the kibbutz saw us as a group, not individuals. We worked hard in our different departments but this was not acknowledged by the members. I began working with the newly introduced mushroom growing. It was hard work and long hours. Just three of us cultivated and grew the mushrooms in a converted chicken house. They had to be cared for intensively. Temperature and water control were critical. Once ready they had to be harvested, packed and driven to the airport within hours. They would be shipped to Europe and America. Kibbutz members were required to put in an extra two hours a week in addition to their normal jobs to help with the mushroom harvesting and packing. Few ever turned up to do these limited shifts leaving us three most of the work. While I was doing ten and twelve hour shifts and driving a van load of mushrooms to the airport half asleep, I was still seen by kibbutz members as a trouble maker and lazy. Our reputation stank, yes there had been indiscretions and at times less than acceptable conduct from both sides but nothing we could do now could repair that damage. The kibbutz received money from the Jewish Agency to house us yet unlike the members who had their own houses, we still shared rooms. Kibbutz members had the use of the half a dozen cars for days out or to visit relatives elsewhere in the country. An agreement before the army to give us use of the cars once we returned was reneged upon by the kibbutz. The only time we were allowed was when one night, Yael needed to be taken to hospital and no member was willing to drive her. Members on the kibbutz received a financial allowance and on a Thursday was 'Chaluka' or distribution when food and fruit were handed out to the residents to use at home, a welcome change cooking at home rather than eating in the main dining room. Members received more produce, volunteers less. Although we were prospective members we only received a volunteers allowance. The taste as sour as the lemons we did receive. All was brought to a head when our representative Rita wrote an article for the kibbutz magazine. Filled with false allegations and abuse we were described as lazy and a bad influence on the kibbutz. We were labelled a failure and she hoped the new garin would be more successful. It was only what most of the kibbutz were thinking but she, as our liaison, was supposed to support us. We were all in a no win situation. We didn't want to be there, the kibbutz didn't want us there but whether we left or remained was a decision only the army could make as technically we were still in the army. They said remain. The army was quite adept at keeping everybody miserable.

We spent as little time as possible on the kibbutz. Jo visited Peter, her fiance, in Ra'anana, near Tel Aviv, most weekends. I travelled to stay at Tzuba, or visit Stella and Ossi or stay with other friends. Others too were quick to escape the horrible atmosphere at any opportunity. Technically we were still in the army and needed to be ready for any call up. It was actually a pleasant break when we were called for a weeks training on the Golan. It was good to reunite with other members of the unit. There was a return of the Johhny and Ian show and the Gideon and Eddie Show, just as entertaining as it had been previously. We seemed to spend most of the week smoking and relaxing in our tents. Well it was raining quite a lot. We seemed to spend more time exchanging kibbutz stories than running up and down mountains. It was more like a high school reunion than an army training programme.

August 14th 1986 Back to The Bakum

As I received my discharge papers in the army office the radio played Status Quo 'In the army now'. I burst out laughing. We had travelled back to The Bakum, this time in uniform and we left The Bakum, this time in our civilian clothes. Our field equipment including our weapons had been returned on the Golan some weeks before. The army wanted back only what they had given us except our boots and dog tags. We returned the required pants and shirts retaining the extra ones acquired over time for miluim later. The Bakum had seemed so much bigger when we first arrived. Now we were shuffled one by one into a small cluttered office. Inside I was given my new documents. I watched as the army secretary typed in the booklet, My 'Tudat Shichror' or 'Discharge booklet'. In effect my report card from the army. I finished the army a Private with an armoured personel carrier licence. I was described as 'orderly, able to work in a team, alert and a soldier who fulfilled his commands to a required standard'. I don't think the comments were particularly unique as the two soldiers after me received the same report. I also received my reserve duty booklet. With my boots in my backpack I walked out of The Bakum but not really out of the army, there was annual reserve duty for a month until I was 45.

There were considerably fewer of us. Stuart was dead, Todd back in America. Galore had finished already while Jeremy still had another year. Even though we had come from the relative comfort of the kibbutz rather than the battlefield, the joy was not subdued. That said, much of the time on Kfar Blum had been like a battlefield. My ties, or at least mandatory ties to the kibbutz were now over. It was my choice whether I remained on Kfar Blum, and of course up to the kibbutz whether they wanted me to remain. I knew I would not be returning to Kfar Blum after my trip abroad. In fact none of us, except Jeff, who's girlfriend lived there, planned to stay on the kibbutz. Reuven on Kibbutz Tzuba had made it clear I was welcome there should I decide to live on kibbutz. The other option, a little daunting, was to move to the city and find a job and apartment. For now anyway I was preparing for at least a couple of months away, back to England and a long trip to America.


Chapter 34 Hotel California

August 2nd 1987

A year had passed since my army discharge and my departure from kibbutz. I spent two months in America visiting friends from Year Course in particular. I stayed with Marc and Shannon's best friend Nancy in New York, Sharron in Miami and Stephen in Chicago. I spent a fantastic drug and sex filled week with Shannon in Colorado Springs where even Todd visited for a day. He was now living in Denver. On my arrival at Washington DC airport I phoned Jeremy to be informed his army service had been extended due to his absence after his accident. Jonathan, Jeremy's brother who I had met once on kibbutz when he and Jeremy had visited for a weekend, collected me at the airport taking me to his home. Both he and sister Wendy treated me as royalty during my stay.

Manchester City had reverted back to type and had spent a year in complete turmoil. With a victory over Wimbledon on the opening day of the season things looked promising. Unfortunately the next win didn't come until November, thirteen games later against Aston Villa. By this time the Villa manager was ex City boss Billy McNeil. It was an awful season. City were knocked out of the FA Cup in the third round by United, they scored just 45 goals in all competitions and finished, relegated back into Division Two, second bottom of the table. With just eight league victories and thirty six league goals, their performance was the worst in the league. It was only the three extra points from three more draws that kept them above Aston Villa in bottom place.


I returned to England much in the same mind-set as I had been after my year in Israel. I loved being with my family but felt alienated in England. I knew I would return to Israel but was uncertain of what exactly I would do there. During my time in England I spoke to Peter who had also left the kibbutz and was living in Ramat Gan near Tel Aviv. While many living on kibbutz do so for sound ideological reasons, many live there because they fear moving out into the big wide world. On kibbutz there are no worries about finding a job, finding a house and dealing with the mundane day to day bills. Everything was done for you. I was definitely not returning to Kfar Blum but a kibbutz elsewhere was a possibility. Peter offered me to share his flat in Ramat Gan explaining that getting a job was no problem in the city. My decision was made. I found a job at the Diplomat Hotel in Tel Aviv. Situated on Hayarkon Street along a strip with renowned hotel chains like the Hilton and Ramada I was surprised at the ease of acquiring a job. It did not take long to discover why. The hotel, owned by Haim Shiff was part of a chain of around four hotels. Shiff was later convicted of countless charges including fraud and bribery. Our wages were always at least a month late. Bailiffs spent more time in the hotel than actual guests. Staff without access to cash did not last very long. As a cashier and access to guests bills I joined the other cashiers in taking my wages directly from the cash till. Meanwhile things were not much better at the apartment with Peter. Living with friends rarely works. We clashed most days and when he got himself a dog that ate mostly my shoes it was the last straw. I decided to move out and find a flat closer to the city. The hour commute to Tel Aviv was not the most pleasant either. Shannon spent most of the summer at the flat with me. I don't think I would have survived without her. I was worried I had made a terrible mistake leaving kibbutz and moving to the city. I had a job I wasn't getting paid and a flatmate with whom I was constantly arguing with. Something, everything, had to change.


April 1st 1988 Intifada

On December 6, 1987, an Israeli was stabbed to death while shopping in Gaza. The next day four residents of the Jabalya refugee camp in Gaza were killed in a traffic accident. Rumors that the four had been killed by Israelis as a deliberate act of revenge began to spread among the Palestinians. Mass rioting broke out in Jabalya on the morning of December 9, in which a 17-year-old youth was killed by an Israeli soldier after throwing a Molotov cocktail at an army patrol. This soon sparked a wave of unrest that engulfed the West Bank, Gaza and Jerusalem. Over the next week, rock-throwing, blocked roads and tire burnings were reported throughout the territories. By December 12, six Palestinians had died and 30 had been injured in the violence. The following day, rioters threw a gasoline bomb at the U.S. consulate in East Jerusalem. No one was hurt in the bombing. In Gaza, rumors circulated that Palestinian youths wounded by Israeli soldiers were being taken to an army hospital near Tel Aviv and "finished off." Another rumor, claimed Israeli troops poisoned a water reservoir in Khan Yunis. A UN official said these stories were untrue. Only the most seriously injured Palestinians were taken out of the Gaza Strip for treatment, and, in some cases, this probably saved their lives. The water was also tested and found to be uncontaminated. The intifada was violent from the start. During the first four years of the uprising, more than 3,600 Molotov cocktail attacks, 100 hand grenade attacks and 600 assaults with guns or explosives were reported. The violence was directed at soldiers and civilians alike. During this period, 16 Israeli civilians and 11 soldiers were killed by Palestinians in the territories; more than 1,400 Israeli civilians and 1,700 Israeli soldiers were injured. Approximately 1,100 Palestinians were killed in clashes with Israeli troops.

Peter advertised my room for rent. I was anxious to move on but promised to stay until he found a new flatmate. I had nowhere to go anyway. Niki phoned one morning. She was a twenty year old Catholic girl from Norwich who was in the process of converting to Judaism. She worked as a nursery teacher. We talked on the phone for a while before agreeing to meet at Dizengoff centre in Tel Aviv. Over falafel we hit it off instantly. Unscrupulously we decided to look for a place together and within a few days we had found a first floor apartment on Ester Hamalka Street in the centre of Tel Aviv, just five minutes walk from the Dizengoff Centre. It was perfect. The rent was higher than Ramat Gan but we were closer to the centre and I would save on commuting to work. I could just walk the ten minutes to the beach hotel. Peter was not happy. I was. Apartment sorted it was job time. I applied, and was successful at getting a job, the same role, at the nearby Dan Hotel. I began cutting my days at the Diplomat week by week so after a month or so I was only working a couple of days a month. Nobody who left the Diplomat ever received their final paycheck so to forfeit a wage of three or four days was much better than a full month. The Dan was one of the top hotels in the country. I was finally sorted.

I was late for work as I scrambled out of the apartment towards the hotel. The face walking towards me looked familiar. It was Ian. I hadn't seen him since our army discharge day. It was good to see him and we chatted before arranging to meet up for a drink. He was working in the cafe of the big department store Hamashbir in the nearby Dizengoff shopping centre. I only had a short shift that day and afterwards visited him at the cafe. He was living in the suburbs. We chatted until the cafe closed before returning to my apartment. We laughed at our past days as the hashish smoke filled the apartment.

It was during one of our drug hazed days I opened the letter with the army insignia on the envelope. This was it, my first miluim, reserve duty. I read the letter and burst out laughing. I was being seconded to the military police. As the Intefada continued more military police were needed. I was shortly about to find out my role.

In late 1974, a group affiliated with Gush Emunim named Garin Elon Moreh attempted to establish a settlement on the ruins of the Sebastia train station dating from the Ottoman period. An Israeli cabinet resolution, passed 17–2 with 3 abstentions, found the settlement illegal in 1975. After several attempts to remove residents from the site by the IDF an agreement was reached in which 25 families were permitted to settle in Kadum an army camp south west of Nablus. The small mobile home site developed into the town of Kedumim. The Sebastia agreement was a turning point that opened up the northern West Bank to Jewish settlement. From 1977 on, the government of Menachim Begin strongly backed settlement at Kedumim. Begin visited on May 19 and declared 'We stand on the land of liberated Israel.' In July, his government granted full legal status to Kedumim then numbering around 100 settlers.My first miluim on Kedumin lasted just a week. Three dozen soldiers lived on the settlement whilst learning basic Israeli law. An interesting concept considering the following: Israeli law is incredibly complicated as is is a mish mash of old Otoman law, British Mandate law and modern Israeli law. Add to that my knowledge of Hebrew, quite improved from my early days on the kibbutz but hardly a standard to practice law. Of course, as with all army courses, nobody fails and after a week of unintelligible lectures and copied exam papers, this stone-head was now a military policeman. What a fucking army.

It was strange on the settlement. I had never been on an Israeli settlement in the Occupied Territories before. At Tulkarem during the army we were in an Arab town housed in a police station. Here were a few houses perched on a hill surrounded by layers of barbed wire fencing. Locals moved around the area fully armed with machine guns. Armed convoys brought the settlers in and out of the settlement. What did you call this place? It wasn't a town or really a village but more like a civilian army base. The locals, many British and American ultra religious Jews, had utter contempt for the Arab locals. Others were just average Israelis who took advantage of the right wing governments heavily subsidised housing. They were living in big, three and four bedroom houses, with gardens. They could never afford anything like that in Tel Aviv or Jerusalem. For the ideologists, while the world described the settlers as illegal occupiers of Arab land, they saw themselves as Jews returning to biblical land given by god. I couldn't understand why anybody would live there. The houses were great, large and spacious, and cheap, but they were prisoners. They were surrounded by barbed wire fences and thousands of Arabs baying for their blood. Israelis in the city were often on alert and caught up in terror attacks but on the settlements attacks were a common occurrence. If I struggled with my conscience now, during my second and third miluim I would be ripped apart.

May 7th 1988 10-1

A second season in four years in Division Two ended with a defeat by Crystal Palace. Incredibly City were still averaging crowds of over twenty thousand for home games. During the previous summer Mel Machin replaced Frizzell as City boss. City finished their season back in the second league in ninth place. Their cup performances were an improvement on the previous year making the sixth round of the FA Cup and the fifth round of the League Cup (now named the Littlewoods Cup). There was one extraordinary game during the season. On November 7th 1987 in front of 19,583 fans, Manchester City hosted Huddersfield Town at Maine Road. Despite propping up the rest of the table, lowly Huddersfield could had scored twice in the opening ten minutes. City's Neil McNab opened the scoring in the twelfth minute. Paul Stewart doubled the lead after 29 minutes. By half time Tony Adcock and David White had made it four. Following the break City added another six goals, three in the final five minutes. It was the first time in 25 years that three different players from the same team had all scored hat-tricks in a league game. The game finished 10-1, City's biggest ever win of the century. In true, typical City style, City lost the return fixture 1-0 a few months later.

Chapter 35 The Joker

May 1988- December 1988

Niki lasted only two months at the apartment. An early conversion course came through and she arranged a new flat-mate for me. Nissim was around forty. A native Israeli, a builder who appeared to make vast sums of money before losing it all again on dubious projects. We got on incredibly well especially as a non smoker, he tolerated our weekend drug binges. Ian was now spending every weekend at our flat with Friday and Saturday nights an orgy of booze and hashish. A few months after his arrival our annual lease was up for renewal. The rent was cheap for the area but Nissim reckoned he could do better. Within a week he had done it. A penthouse apartment even closer to the centre of the city, and cheaper. As a builder he had negotiated with the landlord to carry out any repairs needed in the apartment for a cheaper rent rate. Moving in was harder than any army exercise carrying our worldly goods up four floors on a Saturday morning after a drunken Friday night but it was worth the pain. A steak lunch for the helpers went down well.

Nissim put up with a lot from us. I think he liked to father us. We were still naïve to many aspects of life in Israel and he enjoyed watching over us. Although far from religious, he came from a religious Moroccan family and was intrigued by our western debauchery. We rarely ate at home, I mostly ate at the hotel and most of the restaurants nearby offered meal deals that actually made it cheaper eating out. Of course we were no strangers to takeaways. When we did eat at home Nissim cooked. During Passover when bread was unavailable in the Israeli supermarkets we drove to Yaffa and bought Arab pita breads. For the fast of Yom Kippur Nissim made sure we had a fully stocked fridge.

Life was looking good finally. I was enjoying my work at the hotel and even gained promotion to assistant accountant. That was even without a maths qualification. I now worked in the cash office checking bills and doing the cashiers rotas. While I missed interacting with the hotel guests, the extra responsibility and higher pay was welcome. Ian's boss at the cafe, a loud, abrasive American with a sweet English wife and very little business sense, decided to open a Chinese restaurant in the outskirts of the city. In the encyclopedia of business failures, Avram would dominate the pages. During the two months I worked as the only waiter I only served two tables and one of those refused to pay their bill. The other couple received their meal for free following a prize draw at the department store cafe. I worked three nights a week after my shift at the hotel. The restaurant, close to an industrial estate on the outskirts of Tel Aviv had little, if any passing trade. The area was deserted after 6pm. There wasn't a house for miles. I felt guilty taking wages from the guy but not guilty enough to refuse. And I got a free Chinese dinner three nights a week. Shannon visited the country less often and when she did visit she rarely stayed at the apartment. As we grew increasingly distant I found solace elsewhere. Avital, a German volunteer on a nearby kibbutz, Robin, originally from South Africa, now living in Ramat Gan, Ida, from Romania, Adi, also from South Africa, Nurit, an Israeli work colleague, Freda, my Israeli manager, Sigi, a secretary I met during miluim, Osnat, a soldier me and Ian met in a pub one Friday night.

Chapter 36  I Shall Be Released

December 1988


From the watchtower down below

Huddled in your hundreds, hatred grows

There can be no justice, no rights

While the innocents still die


Looking into your cell window

Looking into your hurting eyes

Who can say this is decent?

Who can say this is right?

From the television screen across the room
The shell of a bus, bodies strewn
There can be no justice, no rights
While the innocents die

Barbed wire separates our hopes
I see the pain in your hurting eyes
Bloodshed separates biblical brothers
Do you see mine?

Looking into your cell window
The clock strikes midnight
All alone I guard my fears
Tears trickle from my sorry eyes

One day again we will be brothers
One day again we will stop the fight
Stop, overcome all this hurting
One day we will put it right.

Ketsiot Prison was an Israeli detention facility located in the
Negev desert 45 miles south-west of BeerSheba. It was Israel's
largest detention facility in terms of land area, encompassing
400,000 square metres. It was also the largest detention camp
in the world. During the First Intifada Ketsiot was the location

of the largest detention camp run by the Israeli army. It held three quarters of all Palestinians held by the army, and over half of all Palestinians detained in Israel. In March 1988, around 700 prisoners were transferred from prisons in the Gaza Strip to the newly prepared prison camp. Four days later, Defence Minister Yitzhak Rabin announced that 3,000 Palestinians were under arrest and that a new prison had been opened in the Negev desert According to Human Rights Watch it held approximately one out of every fifty West Bank and Gazan males older than sixteen. Amongst Palestinians it was known as Ansar 3 after a similar prison camp set up in South Lebanon by Israel during the Lebanon conflict. Ketsiot camp was opened in March 1988 and closed in 1995. It was later reopened in 2002 during the second intifada.

It was awful. I had struggled before hand with my conscience. I considered refusing to serve. My life in Israel was finally fantastic save the politics. The country was so massively polarised and split. Half the country, like myself, believed in working towards a peaceful end to the violence and inequalities of the Palestinians. The other half believed in no compromise. I was confused and battling with my conscience. Before the call up I knew what this miluim would involve. Guarding prisoners, some young whose crime had been to resist an occupation. Had I been in their situation I would probably have done the same thing. I was an active member of Amnesty International and the Israeli peace group Shalom Achshav, Peace Now. I supported the rights of Palestinians for their own independence. Yet here I was imprisoning those very people. Of course many of these Arabs had broken the law but these were not the hardcore bus bombing terrorists. They were kids and old men who had thrown rocks at army vehicles. I could have refused to serve here but the army were no mugs.

The few that had refused were jailed for their month's miluim then recalled a couple of months later. Again they refuse, again they are sent to army prison. The months salary of the soldier is covered by the army, unless that month is served in prison. With rent to pay, family to feed, there are only so many months you can go without a wage. The soldiers know this and refusals are rare. The army know the dilemma of the soldiers and use these tactics to stop the dissent. In addition I wanted to serve to show the prisoners that not all Israelis were tyrants. I wanted to be fair and decent. And as a writer I wanted to see and experience all of this for myself. Maybe I just thought this to justify my cowardice at refusing to serve. I don't honestly know.

True to form the army had found another desolate spot for a camp or prison. Out of the surrounding desert were tents surrounded by wire fencing surrounded by more wire fencing. The only structures higher than the fencing were the water towers dotted around the camp. It was hot and dusty. We guarded four at a time. Myself, Sharon, Ely and David stuck together. We had been together for the study week at Kedumin where we had grown friendly. We were all from Tel Aviv or the surrounding suburbs. Ely and David were both married with children. Sharon, like myself, free and single. He was the youngest of the four of us. All had jobs in the city. I got on best with Ely. Slightly overweight with John Lennon circular spectacles he was the intellectual among us. His command of English was excellent. We would spend much of our time, whilst guarding, struggling with the New York Times crossword reproduced weekly in the Israeli English language daily newspaper, The Jerusalem Post. It was through the crossword we met Miray.

Miray was a Palestinian my age. I was an Israeli. We were not allowed to talk to each other. That was a formal order from our officers and an unwritten rule from the inmates. He would often spend his time sat alone near the fencing cleaning and painting stones. It was a few days before he spoke to us. Struggling with a particular difficult crossword clue Miray, asked, in near perfect English, if we needed help. Prisoner and guards on their respective sides of the fence moved closer to each other. The three of us began chatting forgetting about the crossword puzzle. His crime, he told us, was to be arrested for throwing stones at an army convoy some months before. He did not deny the charge and was waiting for his army trial. It would be conducted by an army committee with evidence given by the army prosecution. As it later turned out he was found guilty but the six months he spent in detention was deemed punishment enough and he was released after his trial, six months after his arrest. Miray was more nervous talking to us than we were talking to him. He was afraid of being seen as a collaborator.

It was early morning on our second day we experienced the tent searches. Three officers arrived at our post. The inmates noticed the officers and knew what was happening. Prisoners began running between the tents. One of the officers began laughing. 'They're running home' he said. He explained that some had been there for months and a few had become quite lonely. Relationships had formed and while it was frowned upon by the other prisoners, some did spend the night with their new partners. With the arrival of the officers they knew a tent search was on and they must return to their own bed before the search. The gates were opened and we walked into the first section. The prisoners were ordered to line up outside their tents. David and an officer stood outside watching the prisoners while we entered the tents. We were searching for banned materials not that I was certain what was banned. Obviously home made weapons but the officer confiscated a picture of the Al Asqa mosque in Jerusalem.

The smell was putrid, dirt and sweat. The limited space was filled with garbage. There were mosques crafted out of egg cartons and cigarette packets. There were notebooks in Arabic, Hebrew and English. This was as much a school as a prison. There were rocks that had been sanded down and painted. Images of the Palestinian flag, clenched fists and guns. Real contraband was also found, several home made knives and nails. I felt dirty after the hour long search. That said the searches were important for everybody's safety, not least the inmates. Although knife attacks on other inmates were extremely rare and I never experienced one, they did happen.

We tried our best to be decent guards. We treated our prisoners with respect to the best of our ability. With Miray we discussed everything twenty-somethings discussed. Football, rock music, girls, politics. We had more in common that the political differences that had erected the fence between us. He gave me a stone he had painted. A picture of two hands held together with an inscription in Arabic. 'To Johnny, friends in peace one day'. I was touched. Maybe I had made a difference afterall. Before our departure myself and Miray exchanged phone numbers. He was released shortly after we departed. Nissim was not too happy when Miray phoned the apartment and I explained who he was. Ian thought a was a soft loony liberal. I met with Miray in East Jerusalem. Ely joined us as we sipped coffee and chatted. Perhaps it was more symbolic than anything else. It wasn't easy for him and he spent most of the time nervously looking around. We were not there to change the world or build a peace treaty. We were three friends drinking coffee. We only met the once and I never heard from Miray again.


## Chapter 37 My Ever Changing Moods

February 1989

Camp Ofer was originally founded in December 1968, at the location of a former Jordanian army base from before the Six Day War of 1967. It was named after Zvi Offer the commander of the Haruv Reconnaissance Unit who was killed in action earlier in the same year. The prison was built in the base in 1988, after the onset of the First Intifada Following the Oslo Accords and the numerous prisoner releases of 1995, Ofer's remaining prisoners and detainees were moved to Megiddo Prison, and Ofer was closed. Ofer Prison formerly officially known as Incarceration Facility 385 is located in the West Bank between Ramallah Beituniya and Givat Ze'ev, It is one of three facilities of the same nature, including the Megiddo and Ketsiot prisons. Ofer Prison is run by the Israel Prison Service and like the other two facilities, used to be operated by the Israel Defence Forces Military Police. When under IDF control, it was capable of holding up to 800 prisoners, both tried and those under administrative detention.

The shrill of the clock at six a.m. must have woken half of Tel Aviv. I rolled out of my bed and into my army uniform in almost one action. The boots were tight, the badly ironed uniform fitted well. I left a note for Nissim 'Off to the war, see you in a couple of weeks'. Although we had given our equipment back at the end of our service, we had acquired extras along the journey, not least the army work pants with extra pockets and more importantly on this chilly morning, a heavy green coat. I was nervous but far less anxious than I had been on my first day at The Bakum. I was grateful I had packed my bag the night before. I sipped my coffee as I checked the contents, not that I was totally certain what I would need.

My confidence grew a little as I walked to the local bus stop. I was a real Israeli now doing what real Israelis did. I had been given plenty of support from my work colleagues before the weekend, not least from my boss Avi. We had often been at loggerheads over various issues at work but the Friday before my departure he had slapped my back, smiled and wished me 'Ba'hatslacha' or 'Good luck'. I boarded the local bus at the stop outside Dizengoff Centre. Two workmen got on the half empty bus with me. I strolled towards the middle of the bus with my kitbag thrown over my shoulder. I remembered my first ride on a bus with my large bag, how I had almost decapitated all my fellow passengers. Now I negotiated the trek through the aisle with skilful ease. I could just about hear the music on the radio. The clock struck the hour as the driver turned up the volume. All bus drivers did this. I wasn't sure if it was compulsory for bus drivers to turn up the volume when the news came on the radio. Israeli's could miss out on the latest Paul Weller hit but never the news.

'Kol Yisrael me Yerushalaim, heney ha hadashot, The voice of Israel from Jerusalem, here is the news, Sgt Avi Sasportas was kidnapped by terrorists while hitchhiking at the Hodaya junction' (He was shot dead, his body, which had been buried at the Givati junction in southern Israel, was discovered on 7 May 1989). I looked at the other passengers. There was shock on their faces. Yet another attack on Israeli's yet the hurt and the shock never diminished. I saw a passenger looking at me in my uniform. She smiled at me, like a loving and concerned mother smiling at her departing son. As she passed me to get off the bus, she touched my shoulder, looked me in the eye and muttered 'Be careful'. For all the political divisions, the deep polorisation, we cared deeply for each other.

I lit another Noblesse cigarette as I waited at the collection point. Good job I had brought a few packs with me. One by one my new friends and colleagues from the course a couple of months previously began to arrive. I nodded in acknowledgement. It was too early really to begin a fully cohesive discussion. We boarded the dilapidated Egged bus seconded by the army. I sat next to the window, Sharon, an Israeli my age, sat next to me. We chatted a little but mostly I just stared from the window. Built up Tel Aviv soon became open farm land and within a few minutes we had crossed the green line into the West Bank. The smooth asphalt highway became rocky uneven narrow streets. As the Rolling Stones on the radio were mid song, a small rock hit and cracked the bus windscreen. This was followed by a hail of rocks from the side of the street. The bus driver sped up dramatically and most of us hit the floor. The officer on board shouted for the driver to stop so he could give chase to the youths but the driver ignored the order. He just wanted out of there as quickly as possible. I couldn't have agreed more with his choice of action. The bus driver seemed to leave his foot on the gas pedal even on the tricky bends and turns. Within a very short time we pulled up to the prison gates and the large sign 'Welcome to Kastel'.It took a good ten minutes for the guard to open the twenty foot high, steel gate. Not too reassuring considering we were sat outside, a sitting target and had already been stoned by the locals.

We went straight to lunch, army lunch and a chicken leg and some rice washed down with piss weak juice. Some things never change in the army. I missed the hotel. I even missed

Lebanon where the army food was both tasty and plentiful. Our living quarters contained around twenty bunk-beds and appeared more squalid than the prison cells. The prison was an old fort but the Israeli owners had done building expansion. The building appeared far more intimidating than the soldiers occupying it. Section A housed less prisoners than Section B. I thought it resembled an American police station. Well I had never been in an American police station but it looked similar to those portrayed in the TV cop shows. The upper floor housed the regular soldiers, their offices, a synagogue and a TV room where the television never seemed to work. Downstairs were the cells. You entered the building and were faced with a raised, square reception area. It was completely surrounded by high metal fencing with a metal gate door at the rear. The desk, it's draws filled with packs of very cheap cigarettes, was as big as any of the dozen cells. At the rear of the lower floor were the prisoners kitchens. They cooked their own food. The cells were small and the dozen or so mattresses crammed inside left no vacant floor space. Section B was outside and three enclosures each housed around fifteen tents. They too were filled to bursting. You could not get a cat in let alone swing the poor bastard. Our briefing by the camp commander was relatively brief. He spoke softly explaining there were around three hundred prisoners. Most had yet to be tried and were in detention until their trial. That could take as long as six months. It was stressed we treat the prisoners with dignity but be aware some were there for terrorism offences. Again the officer was considerably younger than the soldiers he commanded but like my officer in Lebanon and unlike Yuval, he appeared to respect this. He talked to us with respect. We were split into two groups and then into sub groups. I stayed with Sharon and two others from the course, Ely and

David. We left the room and headed for our first watch at Section B.

We were greeted at the guard post by a loud cheer from the standing guards. Their month was now over and they could return to their civilian lives. For a few minutes the old guard passed on a few basic tips before calling out several numbers. The prisoners called walked over to the wire fencing. 'Watch these bastards or they'll eat you alive'. He then waved them away. One prisoner stood firm staring deep into the guards eyes. The guard slashed the fence with his stick. The whole fence shook in anger. The prisoner walked backwards to his tent without looking away from the guard. Terror and hatred in both sets of eyes.

The four old guards departed laughing as we were left with two hundred Arab prisoners and a golden sunset. We sat on an old bench covered by what looked like an old bus shelter. The evening seemed to drag. Myself and David made our first patrol of the perimeter of the area. I was shocked by the self inflicted filth. Food discarded around the tents was now invaded by flies. We called for five prisoners and handed them a brush each. They were instructed to brush and clean around the tents. I had given my first order. I am not sure who this was to benefit, the prisoners who would get a clean camp or myself the guard. There was nothing to do most of the time especially as almost all of the prisoners were in their tents. Ely wandered off back to our room before returning with a box containing a kettle, coffee, sugar and a backgammon set. Now we were ready for action. There was no real hurry returning to the dormitory after the five hour shift. There was nothing to do there either. Prisoner meal times were a military exercise. Ten prisoners, selected by the inmates, were escorted by two soldiers to the kitchens. Laden with pots and pans they were marched with breakfast for their fellow prisoners. It certainly looked more appetising than our food. The ten were cheered as they moved between the sections serving the food. Within an hour it was all over and breakfast eaten, utensils collected, it was back to the boredom.

My weekend home was spent with nineteen year old Sigi, a secretary from the office upstairs. With Ian visiting for the weekend with his latest date and Nissim entertaining his married mistress, the flat resembled a brothel. Friday night beers, hash and sex followed by more of the same Saturday night were a welcome break from the Kastel prison. On my return to the prison myself and Ely requested a move to Section A indoors. It was easier as the prisoners were hidden from view by the metal cell doors. The prisoners in Section A were entitled to one hour exercise per day but that rarely happened. I took control of the exercise rota and was blatantly biased with my choices of cells for exercise. The better behaved the cell occupants the more exercise and shower privileges. Naturally the prisoners were pissed off to say the least at being there. Most had attitude but were able to manage it. Those that couldn't found themselves without privileges. In a dispute between soldier and inmate, the inmate always came out loser. The inmates had one spokesman, one united voice, one united aim and slept with one united dream, that of freedom in their own country.

There was one prisoner alone from the crowd on the basketball pitch where the prisoners exercised. I watched through my Raybans, sitting on a plastic chair as one lone individual stood in the corner. The other prisoners milled around in small groups chattering between themselves. I called him over and he nervously walked towards me. He barely looked in his teens.

'Do you speak Hebrew?' I asked him

'A little', he replied

'What about English?'

'A little more' he answered in English.

'What is your name?' I asked softly

'Kahil' he answered.

He told me he was fifteen but I didn't think he was that old. He looked more thirteen or fourteen and terrified. He began telling me his story quite freely but suddenly stopped and turned around. Most of the other prisoners were now watching him. He became afraid. There could be nothing worse than being suspected of collaborating with the enemy. He claimed soldiers had stormed his house in the middle of the night and he had been arrested for stone throwing. He said he had been dragged from his bed half naked to the police station and then on to here. As with every prisoner anywhere in the world, nobody is ever guilty but I believed Kahil. I felt sorry for the child, he was completely out of his depth here. The other prisoners used Kahil to the limit, especially his cell mates. Any request for extra cigarettes or other minor treats were requested by Kahil and almost always granted. None of the other inmates used his relationship with me as a threat. He was too young and inexperienced to pass on any information and my sympathy for him gained them extra rations and exercise.

We dodged even more rocks on our way home for leave. The stone throwers knew we were on our way back home and wouldn't risk that leave by engaging in a fight. We simply sat on the bus floor and waiting until we passed through the storm. Within the hour I was back in Tel Aviv visiting Ian at the cafe. I couldn't be bothered changing out of my uniform. We sipped coffee, I requested it be complimentary for soldiers. Ian agreed. We arranged to meet up for a long, drunken night on the town. I returned to the apartment throwing my dirty uniform in the machine. Shit, on kibbutz they did this for you. The evening passed with much laughter, Goldstar beer and frivolity. I returned to the apartment with Osnat who gave everything. Osnat, Ian and Nissim all departed for work and I enjoyed the quiet. I set about cleaning the apartment following the previous nights debauchery. I wondered how Nissim put up with us sometimes. I sorted my bag ready for my return to Ketsiot. I was now halfway through. As the bus weaved its path through the Tel Aviv early morning, Dire Straits 'Brothers in arms' rang out loud through my walkman headphones.

We arrived back at the prison to find the entire prison population on hunger strike. It appeared this was not a unique event and the officers appeared only slightly concerned. It was only the first day and usually ended after a couple of days. If it went any longer and the top authorities were required to visit then it would get serious. Myself and Ely dropped our bags in the living quarters and walked around to inspect the troubles more in curiosity than believing we could actually solve anything. The inmates sat in their tents in complete silence. Their food remained in the containers touched only by the resident flies. The officer called over a prisoner spokesman who complained they were being given insufficient food. They demanded extra rations and of course they wanted the food that had been sat in the sun all morning replaced. Their rations were already double that of the soldiers and I felt angry at the blackmail. The officer was terrified the incident would escalate. The prisoners in Section A appeared a little less militant than those in Section B. Section B prisoners spent the most part of the next day on numerous roll calls. The roll calls took a lot longer than usual as the guards conveniently kept losing count. Tent searches were stepped up. Floodlights were left on all night and the radio played music much louder than normally. The prisoners slept little if at all. The following morning the inmates could barely stand during morning roll call. There were no more hunger strikes during our service.

Family visits were incredibly important to the prisoners and in the days up to visit day the inmates were on their best behaviour. I was posted on an entry gate along with an intelligence officer. By 6am there was already a crowd of families outside the gates of the prison. Many had brought food and drink, for themselves before the gates opened and for their relatives inside. There was even an ice cream van parked outside. Visiting time arrived and the visitors pushed forward like cattle. Each visitor was searched and checked. I searched the visitor and their bags while the intelligence officer checked the I.D. on the computer print out of wanted criminals. The officer told me there were instances where visitors were wanted by the authorities but still visited family members at prison. They came as visitors and ended up as guests. The intelligence officer was aggressive towards the visitors confiscating countless items from the visitors. He told them they could collect the items after the visit but strangely neither the officer nor the possessions were around after the visit. The visitors were led to a secure area to wait for their loved ones. Moments later the first batch of prisoners arrived. Through a wire dividing fence they laughed, ate, kissed and smoked. There was the occasional outburst from a family outside the area when informed their relative would not be receiving visitors. Some had made a long and expensive journey to the prison in vain. I was deeply upset by the whole process. The only comfort was seeing Kahil with his family. It was the first time I had seen him smile.

Visit over, the prisoners were returned to their cell or tent after a thorough search. Little was allowed through. I was amazed at what had been smuggled through the barrier fence during the visit. The following day the inmates received another visit, this time from the International Red Cross. Three Swiss men moved from section to section handing out pens, writing books, board games and even one hundred pairs of sunglasses. They collected hastily written letters to their families. One official stared at me with disgust. I was angry he had judged me without knowing me. I resented the conclusions he had made about me without knowing the facts or my feelings. I too did not want to be there. I too did not agree with six months detention without trial nor with holding young kids. By now I was bitter and angry. I was angry at the Swiss Red Cross guy, angry at the Arabs, the Israeli's, angry at everyone. I lit a cigarette and looked to the sky for an answer. None came.

The days passed slowly and I switched often between the two sections to alleviate the boredom. Alone on night shift in Section A I spent the night writing or thinking. I wondered at the cost of this whole thing, financially and in human misery. Between the hourly walk around the closed block I even passed some time playing backgammon against myself. I continued my shift into the next day. In the morning an officer arrived with a list of forty prisoners to be moved on. They would be replaced by the fifty sat handcuffed on a bus outside. The process was busy and appeared chaotic although it did alleviate the boredom. The departing guests were brought to Section A along with their limited belongings. For a few it would be home, for the majority a different prison. Each was searched several times before being handcuffed and helped on to a waiting bus. Once all were evacuated the new arrivals were brought inside. Most were frightened and in shock. They sat on the floor outside the office for some time before exchanging their clothes for prison clothes and getting their medical checks from the army doctor.

It was in the early hours of the morning when I was called to help in front of Section A. I turned the corner of the building to see fifteen Arab prisoners lying face down on the ground spread eagle with the hands tied behind their backs with cable ties. The soldiers were shouting, the prisoners were screaming. The blindfolded prisoners were helpless. A couple of hours before they were the heroes of the revolution as they launched stones and rocks at Israeli soldiers and settlers. Now they cowered in fear. They stood cold, frightened and humiliated as the soldiers laughed at their misery. I felt sick. The humiliation lasted almost two hours before the prisoners were finally put into their cells and relative safety.


Chapter 38  Say it Ain't So Joe

March 1989


Look into the skies

What do you see?

An old man looking down upon us?

Created by you and me

We wrote ourselves our holy books

In Arabic, Hebrew and Latin

Told ourselves we were the anointed ones

Promised the desert sands

So we built up our armies
Taught our children the sacred tales
We sharpened our rusty swords
Ready to cut into the infidels
And we believed our cause righteous
As we waged Jihad and Crusade
And war and torture and occupation
All in our Lords name

We prayed for our salvation
To Jesus, Allah, to the almighty
We prayed for our enemies' destruction
We changed our accounts of history

We stoned the non-believers
The scientists and sceptics
Changed the rules when it suited
Still we burned the witches
Whatever your God, Whatever your belief
Don't look above to the skies, The only God lies inside deep.

I walked towards the Section A building for my last night at the Kastel hotel. I climbed the three steps into the building. To my right was the radio and communications room, to my left the officers room. Both were empty at this hour. It was just before ten and I was quite happy doing the night shift until 6am. The prisoners had all had their toilet breaks and were safely locked back in their cells. There would be no reason for the cell doors to be reopened until the morning. Should there be an emergency extra help could be summoned within minutes. I was probably safer here with a hundred or so Arab prisoners than out on the streets of Israel.

I walked the corridor hearing the odd voice from the cells. They weren't overly noisy and left them to it. I returned to my desk and began writing home but it was useless. The words struggled to flow and I was too depressed to force them. Any sign of depression would only worry my family back in England. I knew how these guys here felt. After much fiddling with my pen I finally got back up taking two packs of cigarettes from the desk draw. I walked back along the corridor to cell ten. I opened the small hatch and peered inside. A dozen set of eyes looked towards me. They weren't used to after hours visits. A voice from the back spoke, 'Want to sleep in here tonight Mr. Johnny?'. I declined the offer. Kahil lay at the side of the cell smiling. I threw the two packs of cigarettes towards him. He caught them better than any English cricketer. I knew he would give them away, I knew he didn't smoke but at least he would find favour from his fellow inmates.

'Anyone got a backgammon set I can borrow?' I asked the crowd.

A set was passed forward and I thanked them promising to return it in the morning. I returned to the desk but still couldn't concentrate. This place had made a huge impact on my life in Israel. I opened the game and closed it again. I picked up the phone and requested a line out from the operator. We chatted, or more accurately, flirted. She was finishing her shift and so left the line open for me. I called everywhere except England. I called Stella, Joanne, Ian and Freda in Israel, I called friends in America. Midnight came and went and still I couldn't settle. I walked back to cell 10. I opened the viewer and peered in. most were asleep but Kahil and a couple of others were still awake.

'So you do want to join us then' said one voice.

Tears were filling my eyes as I spoke. ' It is my last night here. I just want to say I am sorry for all this shit. I stand here breaking the law by talking to you but at least I have a country. I share your desire for a homeland, a country of your own. I understand a lot of what you do and would probably do the same myself if I were in your shoes. In the end we have to sort this out. We have to stop killing your children, you have to stop killing ours. This is not right for anybody, you or us.'

I looked around the room and saw just sad, angry children. I saw pain and felt pain. I saw sadness and felt sadness. I felt broken. Kahil stood up and walked towards the cell door. He climbed over sleeping bodies. Others that were awake moved forward too. He spoke softly, the first time he had done so since that first day on the basketball court.

'I am Christian, they are Moslems, you are a Jew but we are all humans. We all have feelings of fear and joy. You are a good man. One day there will be a Palestinian state either next to your state or instead of your state but I truly hope it is next to your state. You shall come to my house as a guest and sit in my chair and eat at my table as my guest. I see your pain here and you see mine. Before I came here all of Israel was my enemy, now I see different. Go in peace my friend.'

I had heard the words I had wanted to hear, the words of reason and hope amid this horror, the words of maturity and reason from a child. I returned to my desk and began to write as the tears dropped heavily onto the notepaper.


I look into the tiny window

How it makes me sad

the pains we are all feeling

the dreams we used to have

midnight arrivals still in night clothes

a heavy cross we must all share

what hope for all our children

when will we start to care?


The bus to take us back to civilisation and bringing our replacements arrived shortly after breakfast. I don't think I had spoken a single word since my guard shift had ended. I felt empty and broken. This was not the country I had loved and respected. I had said this some time before after the way we had been treated following Stuart's suicide. Then I was willing to give it a second chance. Now I was not so sure.

I showed Nissim the advert in the newspaper. A Peace Now march on the West Bank. He smiled. He knew what I was thinking.

'You wanna come with?' I asked

'I'll see you if you get back.' he replied.

That was a no then. Nissim didn't do politics. I remembered some months before talking politics with him. He was born in Israel of Moroccan parents. Moroccans had an unfair reputation for being tough, gangland types. 'Sakin ba gav, knife in the back' I would joke with Nissim sometimes. 'Better than a wimp Ashkenazi' he would joke back. I had always assumed Nissim would vote for the right wing parties.

'What makes you think I don't vote Labour like you' he asked

'Do you?' I asked surprised

'It depends. I don't do the politics of settlements, peace and all that, they are all liars and full of shit. I look at the economy and who will make me richer. Sometimes it's Likud, sometimes Labour.'

I was surprised. Most Israeli's looked to security and who, if any, would bring peace to the country. Nissim didn't trust anybody to do this so voted for his pocket. He didn't trust the Arabs any more either. He watched the news for the financial reports less than the latest terror attack or army incursion. He had lived and worked for several years in Holland and knew 'Western life'. Like most Israelis he wanted that life there in Israel and tried his best to live it. Family stories of Jews living under Arab rule were at best uncomfortable, mostly harrowing. I never heard his parents story but heard of others from Egypt, Syria, Iraq and other Arab countries who suffered anything from victimisation to torture. For Nissim the past was important, his family heritage was important but he wouldn't let it rule his life.

Another weekend early start. Another walk through the streets of Tel Aviv at 6am towards the bus stop. And after a night of very heavy drinking I left Ian and Nissim in the apartment as, extremely hungover, I headed for the local bus and an opportunity to try and do the right thing. We were around fifty strong as we marched towards the village of Beit Sira near Ramallah in the West Bank. The Peace Now demonstrators, flagged by army soldiers, were attempting to reach the village and meet up with local peace supporters. It was all symbolic as there was no way the army was going to let us meet up. As we crossed the fields an officer called on us to halt the march and return to our waiting bus. We were still a few kilometres from our destination. Someone starting running forward and then everybody followed.

Two days before I had been a soldier guarding Palestinian prisoners. Now I was an Israeli citizen being chased through a field by the very same army. It was perverted. Our break-out was as symbolic as our aim of reaching the Arab village. After a few yards we stopped running and collected together. We were addressed by an army officer who appeared sympathetic to our cause but obliged to prevent us going any further. There was no violence especially as the Israeli press were present.

My relationship with Nissim had become a little strained by now too. He was involved in several work projects including building work renovating properties and working with a dance company where he was, for want of a better term, the roadie. I thought that a friend and business colleague of his was mistreating his wife but Nissim appeared to side with him. I felt terrible for the girl and urged Nissim to at least say something but he wouldn't. Perhaps I was wrong, perhaps I had misinterpreted the situation but I still felt upset and uncomfortable.

I entered the Dan Tel Aviv hotel through the employee door at the back as usual. I looked at the beach and the Mediterranean sea before I entered. So close to the beach yet I so rarely visited I thought. I made a pledge to myself to visit more often. I hadn't seen the morning newspapers and was somewhat confused by a few of the comments made by work colleagues as I made my way to my office. Avi and my two other work mates were already at their desks. Avi threw a copy of the Israeli language newspaper Yediot onto my desk, then a copy of the Jerusalem Post. The front page displayed a photograph of the previous days Peace Now demonstration. A group of protesters talking to an army officer. My photograph had made the front page of the newspapers. I felt quite proud but Avi did not share my pride. My two work colleagues remained silent as Avi launched into a tirade of abuse. Apparently I was everything from a left wing softy to a traitor. This was the last straw. Issues debated on the streets of Britain pretty much involved lifestyle issues. Debates on the streets of Israel involved life and death. There was no country on the border of Great Britain hell bent on its annihilation. Israel had over half a dozen just a missile strike away. All this made for heated and highly aggressive arguments from the Israeli parliament to the streets and offices of the nation. Everybody had an opinion, a very strong opinion, on everything. With the country split down the middle and elections always creating hung parliaments ultra extreme left and right wing political parties inevitably held the balance of power. A party with just one or two members of parliament could often bring down a government. School history books were constantly rewritten depending on the political viewpoint of the Ministry of Education. Two brothers, two years apart at school could learn two completely different accounts of a military operation carried out in the war of independence. The victors always write the history books, whatever the truth.

Israel was screwed up. Like a child that had an abusive upbringing, Israel bared the scars of an abusive history. The Holocaust did more damage than kill six million Jews. It left scars on the European Jews in Israel that survived. It caused resentment amongst the Sephardi Jews of Israel who also suffered, not by the Nazis but at the hands of their Arab hosts. They complained that their hurt wasn't recognised. Then there are the religious Jews who are happy to live in Israel, accept government handouts to sustain their Yeshivas, to support them while they learn the bible for the hundredth time rather than work and pay taxes. And when the hard working, tax paying, army serving secular Israeli Jew wants to go out for a beer on a Friday night, the Rabbis demand the law closes all bars and entertainment on the Sabbath. The political structure of Israel gives a few religious zealots power over the entire population. I was all for a Jewish state but I was more for a free Jewish state. A nation where religion and state were separate, where the religious could pray all day if they wanted but after they had defended their country or paid for the council to remove their garbage. I wanted a country where non religious could drink a beer on a Friday night, where gays were not pelted with rocks, where lovers who were not orthodox Jews, could marry without having to hop on a boat to Cyprus.

I worked through the morning in complete silence. My lunch break could not come soon enough but I wasn't willing to wait. It was barely 10am as I walked across the road and ordered a beer at the cafe. I watched the waves crash against the harbour rocks and on to the shore. It was already hot as sweat made marks into my shirt under the arms. The beach was quiet save for a few joggers and an elderly man doing exercises. It was all so peaceful. This could have been Spain, the south of France, the Italian Riviera. It was until you read the newspapers or watched the television news and witnessed yet another bus bombing or Palestinian rock thrower being shot dead. Israel did that to you. It made you marvel at the beauty of the country, wonder at the achievements of the people. Desperate Jews from Kiev to Khartoum, who arrived with nothing but the shirts on their backs. They turned malaria swamps into farms. They held off and beat back millions of Arab soldiers. They invented the Intel computer chip. Israel did all that yet made you despair too. It made you despair that with all those achievements it's people still could not do politics, that all that was seriously jeopardised by the fighting between left and right, religious and secular. I was due back at my desk but first I had somewhere to go. I walked along Ben Yehuda street to Kahol and Lavan, Blue and White, Travel Agency. Half an hour later I walked out of the travel agents with a flight ticket back to England.

Free Bird (Epilogue)

As I walked away
From the tears and the pain
Maybe I had surrendered
struck by the hand of Cain

Your cruel words cut deep
leaving scars to this day
The foundations rock in your ivory tower
Its easy to judge from so far away
My footprints in the sand carve deep
Minutes later the tide erases any trace
You may forget I was ever here
But your love will never be replaced

I watched the sun go down one last time
losing more than a single tear
My possessions loaded on a truck
But my heart will always remain here
I followed the tracks of the rainbow
Living from morning to days end
Love brought on the back of a desert wind
Then lies bleeding at storms end.

Shannon had called me a traitor when I told her I was returning to England.

'At least I tried' I told her. But I was still hurt.

I was showered with gifts and praise by my work mates at the hotel. I left with a tearful good-bye from Stella and Ossi, Jo and Jeremy. Ian had already returned to England. I left without saying good-bye to Nissim, and later apologised for that inappropriate behaviour. Israel had given me my independence and some incredible friends. The army had given me pride and shame, joy and pain. The army gave me friendships,relationships and love for Jo, Todd, Jeremy and Ian. For that alone it was worth that pain.


On September 11th 1989 I boarded an EL AL plane back to Manchester. I was heading back to England but I wasn't sure I was 'going home'.

## The Rainbow

Tears good-bye, blue and white jumbo flight, porno magazines inside the times, the grand design. Whisked through passport control, badge saying I've come home, home alone, the tears all gone.

Hiding bikes on house roofs, any love you choose, beers by the river, salad again for dinner. Dropping apples on American queens, love behind a cotton screen, a box filled with dreams.

Yellow desert bird in hand, lizards dance in the sand, not quite the beach holiday, no rain again today. Crawling through thorns, huddle together from the storm, cry not in English, too long the wish list.

Army medical tests, the false taste of success, nobody ever fails, we will prevail. Tears on letters from family, half truths towards immorality, BBC news on the radio, checkpoint outside Jericho

Chocolate milk freezing cold, bus full of snoring soldiers returning home, returning home, returning home little prince painted shirt, everybody hurts, desert patrol on a donkey, a million places I'd rather be.

Manchester city live in Lebanon, night flares over Babylon, guardians of the border, San Francisco on the water, scorpions in our boots, are we still resolute? Banana on toast, battles to boast, beware the memory overdose.

Tears good-bye, blue and white jumbo flight, photos of our times, farewell to the grand design. A rainbow follows the heavy rain, love follows the deep pain, friendships last forever, our souls bonded together.

# ACKNOWLEDGMENTS

I began writing this book as a diary in 1984 and finally completed this work some thirty two years later. While many of my accounts are fact and accountable, others, especially with the passage of time, may be remembered or interpreted differently by others.

A special thank you to Joanne Ostrin who held my hand through our army and kibbutz days and has never let go since. Her comments, feedback and grammar corrections made this work a more accurate and cohesive book. Thank you also to Todd Ruback whose feedback also helped in completing this book.

As with the lyrics from 'Hotel California', 'You can check out any time but you can never leave', Israel has and always been in my life and will always be so. From my days on Young Judea Year course in 1980 to this day I have enjoyed friendships and experiences that have truly enhanced my life, all forged in Israel. Thank you to Jeremy Welfeld and Ian Lazarus, Stella, Ossi and Ruti Vernik, Stephen Gross and Nissim Boganim. Thank you to Malcolm, Moshe, Jeff, Susan, Erica and all of Garin Nesher. Thank you to the soldiers of Nahal Peh Bet, the Israeli soldiers to Kibbutz Shamir, my miluim colleagues and my fellow workers on Kfar Blum, Hotel Diplomat and Hotel Dan Tel Aviv.

Thank you, my friends.

Because of you, my life is considerably richer.

Lightning Source UK Ltd.
Milton Keynes UK
UKHW011230201118
332641UK00006B/594/P